PRAISE FOR *BROKEN T*

Broken to Safe is a must-read for anyone who wants to create an inclusive workplace. Fay has taken robust research and translated it into easy-to-understand storytelling, with adaptable templates you can bring to your business. Her intellect shines on every page. This book goes well beyond the concept of diversity to belonging: the key to making sure everyone is safe at work. I would urge every CEO, manager and executive to read it.

Tracey Spicer AM,
Author of *MAN-MADE* and multiple Walkley Award winning journalist

We are how we lead. And in the briefest of glimpses into her background in the opening chapter, Fay provides an insight into why she leads with compassion, resilience and determination. A successful employment lawyer of some 20 years, Fay's insights and observations are borne from deep experience. *Broken to Safe* is compelling reading for leaders who need and want to do more for their workplace than merely comply with rules and regulations. Fay's assertion that 'culture is at the heart of change' has never been more true or more challenging to get right. *Broken to Safe* humanises the key risks and opportunities all organisations face and provides a playbook for best practice. I highly recommend it.

Marina Go AM,
Independent Chair, NED and Author of *Break Through*

This book is a must-read for all leaders. It offers a practical roadmap for creating a thriving workplace culture. If you are a leader who cares about your team members, you won't be able to put this book down.

Dr. Kirstin Ferguson,
Author of *Head & Heart: The Art of Modern Leadership*

Fay Calderone

BROKEN

TO

SAFE

Tackling toxic workplace cultures and burnout

First published 2024 by Fay Calderone

Produced by Independent Ink
independentink.com.au

Cover design by Catucci Design
Edited by Brooke Lyons
Internal design by Independent Ink
Typeset in Rotunda Variable by Post Pre-press Group, Brisbane

ISBN 978-1-7635796-0-6 (paperback)
ISBN 978-1-7635796-1-3 (epub)
ISBN 978-1-7635796-2-0 (kindle)

DISCLAIMER

Nothing in this book is intended to constitute legal advice. Readers must not rely on the contents of this book as an alternative to obtaining comprehensive legal advice. You should never delay seeking legal advice, disregard legal advice, or commence or discontinue any legal action because of the contents of this book or in any way treat this book as a substitute to obtaining specific legal advice for issues you are dealing with in your workplace.

CONTENTS

In writing this book, I acknowledge the original storytellers on the land that I write from, the Aboriginal and Torres Strait Islander peoples. I honour their connection to land, waters and communities and pay my respects to Elders past, present and emerging and to Aboriginal and Torres Strait Islander peoples who may be reading this book. Sovereignty has never been ceded. It always was and always will be Aboriginal land.

INTRODUCTION

We live in a world where leaders struggle to attract and retain talent and where humans in our workplaces are burning out. It is troubling how many talented humans we lose, or who fail to thrive in our workplaces due to the systemic structural and cultural issues that present barriers to safe and inclusive participation and progression.

Over the years humans have been subjected to unacceptable levels of bullying, discrimination and sexual harassment that have caused them to leave work. Women in particular face serious structural barriers in 'balancing' family and work life. People who are culturally and racially marginalised, have disabilities, are neurodivergent, suffer from chronic health conditions or escaping family violence also experience barriers to their healthy participation and progression in the workplace.

I was honoured to interview Walkley Award–winning journalist Catherine Fox for this book and will be sharing her insights with you.[1] She made similar observations about the talent we lose unnecessarily due to the failure to address unlawful conduct and other barriers women in particular face at work. She shared:

There are very few women I know who have not run into some form of bullying, discrimination or sexual harassment in their career. They are being overlooked, having their skills completely underestimated, sometimes ignored.

I have worked with some exceptional women. I think that just about all of them at some point have come across this, although many of them have obviously persevered as well. But it is so hard to quantify the loss. People like you and me know it is incalculable. You come across a talented woman that you just happened to meet at a social gathering and think they should have had an amazing career. But something has clearly happened. They do not say much and they're not whinging, but you can just tell something has happened to them and it's such an enormous waste.

The 'something' that has happened to them is often that they have been broken by the workplace due to one or many of the reasons outlined in this book.

There is much more we can do to retain, engage, support, mentor, sponsor and nurture diverse groups of humans in our workplaces. Every one of us can make a change, and collectively we can make a monumental difference. Our nation is built on a rich tapestry of diversity and stories of courage, resilience and determination. Success lies in sharing our stories, learning from them, creating a solid foundation of diversity, embracing inclusiveness in every way, harnessing the strengths we each bring and respecting one another and our unique gifts. Success lies in ensuring humans are safe at work.

Creating safe workplaces

After more than 20 years' practice as an employment lawyer, the thing that fascinates me the most is how it encompasses all that is good and not so good about humans. The highs and lows humans experience in their lives. The fragility and fallibility of the human condition. The consequences of poor choices and lapses in judgement. It all manifests in the workplace and lands on the desks of leaders around the world and, in turn, with us as employment lawyers.

What I remain curious about is the human condition, and why people do the things they do. Is it nature or is it nurture? Are there human traits that lead to dysfunction or does dysfunction arise from the environments we put people in? To what extent can leaders and people and culture/human resources (HR) professionals shape behavioural and transformational change in workplaces?

I never take for granted the privilege to help leaders navigate these matters. It means so much to help them overcome these challenges and use my knowledge, experience, insights and learnings to build safe, inclusive and respectful workplaces. This has become my purpose and now, the purpose of this book.

As I look behind the curtain as a trusted adviser to countless leaders in workplaces large and small, I have developed deep insights into what keeps you up at night as a leader or HR professional.

I know you are concerned about legal risks.

I know you are overwhelmed by the regulatory and compliance burden.

I know you do not want to end up in court.

I know you fear damage to your reputation and that of your organisation.

I know you are under pressure to ensure productivity and financial sustainability.

I know you worry about the health, safety and wellbeing of humans in your workplace.

I know you want your workplace to be safe, healthy and inclusive for humans at work.

I know you struggle to reconcile all the above.

I know that sometimes the above is irreconcilable.

I know you may, from time to time, struggle with the psychosocial hazard the burden of all of this creates for you personally.

In my work I try to provide not only legal advice but commercial, practical and compassionate advice to support leaders with all I have mentioned here. I wrote this book to help leaders and HR professionals address what often feels like overwhelming, conflicting and irreconcilable obligations.

Why I wrote this book

I believe our experiences shape who we are as leaders and humans. My life has undoubtedly driven my purpose to build diverse, healthy and inclusive workplaces and to share all I have learnt along the way, including by writing this book.

My story is of a girl who was born in Australia shortly after her parents, Greek Cypriot refugees, migrated here. It's the story of a girl who grew up in western Sydney and lives with chronic autoimmune disease. It's the story of a girl who had a dream and let nobody stand in the way of realising it. It's the story of a girl turned mother who wants to create a legacy for her teenage boys, to make workplaces safer and more inclusive for them and their generation.

My parents instilled in me at an early age that compassion and respect for and from others is life's most valuable asset. But I also learnt what it means to be resilient. I learnt that when times get tough you need to survive. I observed what it meant to be a superwoman working mother doing it all. I felt the energy and determination my father poured into the family business and the strong enduring connections he built. My parents may not have had the money for private education or time for weekend sport, but they instilled in us a strong work ethic, resilience, values and grit.

I was a sickly child. Having had multiple operations and seen count-less specialists, I finally collapsed at age 13 and was taken to hospital. I was misdiagnosed with pleurisy before a local GP diagnosed Hashimoto's thyroiditis. My thyroid had completely stopped working.

I was nevertheless an enthusiastic and ambitious young woman. I gave 110 per cent to every exam, assignment and task like it was do or die. Everything mattered. I studied career guides from the first year of high school. I planned my courses, my career trajectory, my work options … my life. I was so determined to achieve, to be the best I could be. Always.

Despite my school careers counsellor warning me that few girls from public schools in western Sydney become lawyers, I planned a very specific path to study Human Resource Management and Law as the first in my extended family to obtain a tertiary education. I went on to work in private practice, where I worked on matters for some of the most impressive employers in our country (including a secondment to Nine during Kerry Packer's reign). I was married by 22 and, by 28, when we had saved enough for me to take six months of unpaid parental leave, our first child was born.

When our son was five months, I was due to return to work full-time, but living on the outskirts of the city and wasting almost three hours a day on travelling to the CBD was untenable. When the opportu-nity arose to help build an employment practice in an established commercial law firm in Parramatta, I jumped at it – despite not being sure if it was career suicide or serendipity.

They say fortune favours the brave (and perhaps the hardworking?) and I was promoted to partnership equivalent in an incorporated legal practice at the age of 32. Each step of my career was a building block to my current position as an equity partner with one of Australia's most successful independent domestic law firms.

However, giving 110 per cent to everything comes at a price. Any high-performance coach will tell you no-one can run at that level all the time. The quest for perfection is exhausting and unachievable, inevitably leading to disappointment and burnout.

The harder I tried in work, motherhood and even at the gym the more tired I became. My fitness over the years was not improving, and in fact was getting worse. I was dizzy, breathless and fatigued. My hands ached, my heart raced and my hair started falling out. I put it down to stress, being a tired working mum with a thyroid condition. As it turns out there was a little more going on – a rare autoimmune disease called systemic sclerosis and a few heart complications to go with it. Naturally this rocked me. As I approached my 40th birthday, I was also being investigated for a serious complication with this disease called pulmonary artery hypertension and was devastated to read of the poor outcomes people with it face. Our boys were only six and 11 and I couldn't believe I might not see them as adults; and, as our family's main breadwinner, that I might not be able to support them. It sent me into a self-destructive spiral. What was the point of all the striving, achieving and self-control if I was to succumb to a disease I had no control over?

As I write this six years later, with thanks to the close monitoring and management of half-a-dozen specialists, the worst has not eventuated health wise. The perspective living with chronic illness has given me is the silver lining: it led me to living my purpose of helping organisations build respectful, healthy and inclusive workplaces. I continue to work hard but I reap the rewards of that hard work. Despite countless resolutions to step back and take it easy, truth be known I continue to work too much and am yet to master the art of enough. I am acutely aware of it and working on (in the words of my 12-year-old) the need to 'do better'!

My observations are that, as a society, we are more conscious of the toll excessive working hours and burnout has on us. I am increasingly seeing employers, leaders and industries focusing on this, and laws changing to help us address it. Part of my motivation for writing this book was the ongoing discussions I have with leaders and HR professionals craving practical guidance and advice on addressing psychosocial hazards in their workplaces to ensure their workplaces are safe. It is a brave new world. Employers, leaders and HR professionals are understandably at pains to ensure compliance and manage risk.

I hope this book will help you do better. I hope it inspires you to change your corner of the world by creating a safer, more inclusive and respectful workplace.

About this book

Throughout this book I'll discuss elements of 'box-ticking compliance' but, more importantly, I'll guide you through the steps beyond this – the things you can do to make the humans in your workplace safer and happier, and your life as a leader or HR professional easier. The aim is to make your workplace not only more compliant, but a better place to work, delivering returns for all stakeholders.

This book is not intended to be a 101 crash course in employment law. Instead, I want to help you understand that if you get some fundamentals right, you do not need to spend all your time and energy preoccupied with box-ticking compliance.

Of course, nothing in this book is intended to constitute legal advice. Instead, this book will guide you to know when you should pick up the phone and call a lawyer you trust. For any leader in any business, these times will inevitably arise. You should be prompt and diligent in the way you respond to high-risk situations. That said, the aim of this book is to help you reduce the likelihood they will eventuate in the first place.

In **PART I: BROKEN AT WORK**, we'll explore the myriad issues that create broken humans in your workplace (see Figure 1).

FIGURE 1: BROKEN AT WORK

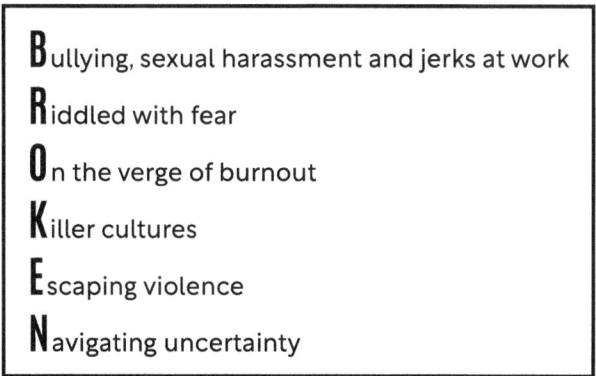

Bullying, sexual harassment and jerks at work

Riddled with fear

On the verge of burnout

Killer cultures

Escaping violence

Navigating uncertainty

These are some of the issues that can lead to dysfunction, misconduct, underperformance, errors, absenteeism, high staff turnover and declining productivity and morale. Eventually, these result in the claims we deal with as employment lawyers including:

- workers compensation claims
- investigation and prosecutions for breaches by regulators including work health and safety (WHS) regulators, the Fair Work Ombudsman and the Australian Human Rights Commission
- unfair dismissal claims
- general protections including adverse action and unlawful termination claims
- applications for stop orders – bullying, sexual harassment and the right to disconnect
- discrimination and sexual harassment claims
- industrial disputes
- breach of contract claims.

PART II: SAFE AT WORK provides detailed guidance on how you can ensure humans in your workplace are safe at work, safe on your watch as their leader (see Figure 2).

FIGURE 2: SAFE AT WORK

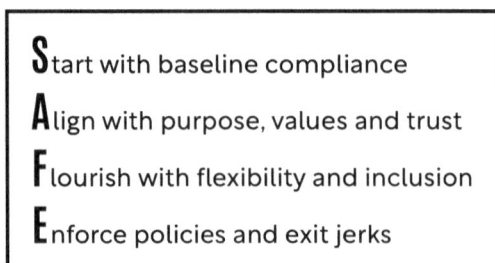

Start with baseline compliance

Align with purpose, values and trust

Flourish with flexibility and inclusion

Enforce policies and exit jerks

This is where the magic happens; where purpose and values integrate with your diversity, equity, inclusion and wellbeing initiatives and you start to experience the benefits of humans who are safe at work.

While the law often feels like a minefield, when we come back to basics the solutions can be quite simple – not necessarily easy to achieve but simple to conceptualise. Psychological safety and trust are fundamental to the creation of a safe, respectful and inclusive workplace where humans thrive, and organisations prosper.

There will always be exceptions. There will always be humans who go rogue. There will always be humans with vexatious complaints that are difficult to reign in. We will never be able to completely avoid disputes and legal claims, but these need not lead us to consume all our time and energy on box-ticking compliance. Your interactions with everyone in your workplace should not be adversely impacted because of the potential for fallout with those who are exceptional, but you must be consistent and robust in managing the exceptions as they arise.

Leading humans is an artform. You need to build trust and guard your values and culture. You need to inspire humans with purpose and action. Inclusive and values-driven leadership is the high watermark you should aspire to, if your goal is to build not only compliant but safe, healthy and respectful workplaces. This is how you capture hearts and minds.

While you must comply with baseline requirements, this book captures the key takeaways that will empower you to be a better, more compliant and inclusive leader or HR professional. It is by no means the holy grail, but it is a pretty good place to start and come back to when things go wrong. (They sometimes will. Such is the human condition.)

In the final chapter of this book, we will work through a case study together. Aspects of this scenario may sound familiar to you; it may be one you have already confronted and perhaps one of the reasons you are reading this book. This case will get you thinking about the challenges you face as a leader or HR professional; the conflicting interests you juggle as you look after the humans in your care. It provides a practical and realistic scenario to help you consider the concepts we will work through in the book. It also gives you an illustrative example of *how* you can practically apply the safe at work principles, and *what* you can do to rescue your organisation.

Earlier in this introduction I shared my story with you. It has shaped me into the lawyer and leader I am, but it is not the focus of this book. I do not hold myself out to be the perfect leader or to perfectly practise everything in this book, but I am trying and learning every day. I am trying to be a better leader and a more curious and well-informed lawyer. I am trying to master the art of enough in a world where burnout is rife, and humans are struggling.

As you read this book, I encourage you to reflect on your own story and consider how it has shaped you into the leader you are, and more importantly the one you want to be. It is brave to be vulnerable. Wear it like a badge of honour. Let your adversity guide you and learn from your experiences. The course of life and leadership never run smoothly. It's what makes us better. With the right mindset, your challenges can make you remarkable. Use your experiences to inspire you to make your workplace safer and more inclusive. Each of us as individuals can help change our corner of the world and collectively, one human, one leader, one workplace at a time, we can make a monumental difference. Godspeed.

Part I

BROKEN AT WORK

Bullying, sexual harassment and jerks at work

Riddled with fear

On the verge of burnout

Killer cultures

Escaping violence

Navigating uncertainty

Chapter 1

Bullying, sexual harassment and jerks at work

A new era is upon us. It's an era in which compliance requirements are more onerous than ever before; consequences for bullying and sexual harassment complaints are more costly than ever; and brand damage to leaders and organisations arising from the transparency of the #MeToo movement has been catastrophic. In this era, to not only thrive, but survive, organisations must embrace diversity, equity, inclusion, belonging and wellbeing and leaders must inspire cultural change.

In toxic and dysfunctional workplaces we observe the victim-survivor of bullying and sexual harassment in one corner. They are rattled at the hands of their perpetrator, and often find it impossible to articulate how they have been reduced to the unsavoury state they find themselves in. In the other corner is the classic workplace jerk: a bully who is also a genius surgeon, a great salesperson, a technical expert, a high-flying professional, a superbly productive line manager, a world-class revenue generator or a charming and dazzling upward manager. They are often considered by the organisation as untouchable, invaluable or even irreplaceable – which is where the danger lies.

Beneath these classic untouchables lies a revolving door of humans who become collateral damage. They're the victims of midnight rants from jerks who hide behind keyboards and shy away from honest and constructive conversations they should have in the light of day. They're the disheartened humans who feel they must move on. Will they complain? Not usually. A disgruntled few will come out all guns blazing, but most will simply leave.

Culture is at the heart of change

To comply with the law, you must develop policies and procedures as a necessary baseline and educate and instruct workers and leaders about the standards of expected conduct, what they must and must not do – but when it's all said and done, culture will eat compliance for breakfast. Contracts, policies and procedures will not protect an organisation that does not – in the way it conducts its business – adopt a zero-tolerance stance against bullying and harassment in any form, at any time. Policies and procedures will not protect an organisation unless they are consistently and indiscriminately enforced.

Culture is now more important than ever as digital media has blurred the boundaries between work and the outside world, and the parameters of behaviour an organisation is looking to regulate become infinite. There was a time when humans worked nine to five and what happened in the office stayed in the office. There was a time when out-of-office interactions between humans were limited to the office party or the occasional get-together between colleagues on a weekend where they might have a quiet chat about a colleague or grumble about a boss over a beer at the pub. Those days are gone. Now, whatever goes on at the office party ends up on social media and often stays there to be seen by an infinite number of individuals.

Transformational cultural change is challenging. The compliance issues are critical: developing of policies and procedures, risk assessments and training programs outlining the required standards of behaviour, unacceptable behaviour and expectations of bystanders is a crucial first step. Workers must be inducted, trained and continuously educated on these requirements, and policies and procedures must be consistently and indiscriminately enforced and reinforced. However, the most successful leaders do not only insist on compliance; they positively embrace diversity and the gifts an inclusive workforce can bring. They create safe workplaces for humans and encourage them to speak up when things go wrong (as they sometimes will). They reinforce core values such as respect and inclusion, with which unacceptable behaviours simply cannot co-exist.

There's an increasing appreciation of the impact of sexual harassment and bullying at work, and the significant cost to the workplace including the cost of turnover, absenteeism and legal claims. This creates further impetus for leaders to stop tolerating the intolerable. Further, the next generation of humans are not prepared to show up, shut up and turn a blind eye to keep the peace or their jobs. They are altruistic, values-driven and not shy to shun jobs and organisations that conflict with their beliefs. They are also not shy to tell everyone about it on social media.

Over the past few years, we have seen unprecedented reports and movements across social and traditional media, including #MeToo and #TimesUp, calling out sexual harassment and sexually inappropriate behaviour at work. This was before the introduction of the *Anti-Discrimination and Human Rights Legislation Amendment (Respect at Work) Act 2022* (Cth) which amended the *Sex Discrimination Act 1984* (Cth) (the *SDA*) – collectively referred to as the Respect@Work laws. These laws aim to finally achieve respect at work by creating a positive duty on organisations to take all reasonable steps to eliminate sexual harassment, sex-based harassment, victimisation and conduct that creates a hostile workplace on the grounds of sex (see the definitions and explanations of these terms in next section).

The Respect@Work laws followed the recommendations of the Australian Human Rights Commission's *Respect@Work* report which said we, as a society, must accept the premise: 'Workplace sexual harassment is not inevitable. It is not acceptable. It is preventable.'[2]

The *Respect@Work* report revealed a harrowing 39 per cent of women in Australian workplaces had been subjected to sexual harassment in the previous five years. Those most vulnerable in our workplaces, including Indigenous and LGBTIQA+ humans, younger workers, those with disabilities, workers from culturally diverse backgrounds or with living arrangements that are precarious or insecure, are even more susceptible.

Similarly, Deloitte's *2023 Gen Z and Millennial Survey* reported more than six in ten Gen Zs (61 per cent) and nearly half of Millennials (49 per cent) had experienced harassment or microaggressions at work in the previous 12 months.[3]

The *Respect@Work* report made recommendations for early intervention – metaphorically, putting a fence at the top of the hill rather than an ambulance at the bottom. We know there are cultural and systemic drivers at play and power disparities that enable sexual harassment. It is recognised we need grassroots cultural change through our education system and communities; to restore the balance of power by increasing regulatory and early interventions measures to protect victim-survivors; to drive personal accountability of individuals to achieve general deterrence; and to embolden organisations to take the power back from sexual harassers by allowing immediate termination of employment for serious misconduct.

The Respect@Work laws echo the accountability-driven laws we already have in relation to WHS (which also applies given bullying and sexual harassment are psychosocial hazards), employee underpayments, migration, whistleblowing and banking executive accountability. Personal accountability drives action and leadership, leadership drives change, and change transforms cultures and achieves deterrence.

Leaders across Australia must now take reasonable and proportionate measures to eliminate sex discrimination, sexual harassment and victimisation, and the Australian Human Rights Commission has the power to scrutinise compliance by investigating workplaces and issuing notices. Unions can also bring representative actions in relation to breaches which increases the risk of leaving these behaviours unchecked on your watch.

The Respect@Work laws seek to drive personal accountability by extending liability to individuals who 'permit' one person to sexually harass another. As a leader you can become an accessory to unlawful conduct if you were aware or should have been aware that unlawful conduct was occurring, or that there was something more than a remote possibility of it occurring and did nothing to address it. The standard you walk past is the standard you accept. This allows dysfunction to perpetuate. Those responsible are now accountable.

The law

The law defines many forms of conduct that are unlawful under state and federal discrimination laws, safety laws and the *Fair Work Act 2009* (Cth) (the *FWA*), as outlined in Table 1. There is an intersectionality between the various forms of unlawful conduct, which often overlap, permeate and perpetuate in toxic and dysfunctional workplaces.

There are multiple risks and exposures for organisations and leaders arising from this conduct in the workplace, including consequences for breaching the *Sex Discrimination Act 1984* (Cth) (the *SDA*), civil penalties under the *FWA*, criminal penalties under WHS laws and personal liability if, broadly speaking, an individual is a perpetrator or an accessory to unlawful conduct.

Leaders and HR professionals must be particularly cautious of accessorial liability provisions in various jurisdictions which can have a low bar at a high personal cost – not only in the form of potential legal liability, as an individual involved in a contravention, but reputational cost for individuals defending such claims.

TABLE 1: UNLAWFUL CONDUCT AND THE LAW

Unlawful conduct	Definition	Relevant laws
Bullying	Repeated and unreasonable behaviour directed towards a worker or a group of workers that creates a risk to health and safety.	• *FWA* – application for orders to stop bullying • State WHS and workers' compensation laws
Discrimination	When a person is treated less favourably than a person who does not have the protected attribute would be treated in the same or similar circumstances (direct discrimination). Examples of protected attributes include race, sex, disability, age, sexual orientation, gender identity, intersex status, marital or relationship status, pregnancy or potential pregnancy, breastfeeding and family responsibilities. Discrimination also occurs when there is a rule or policy that is the same for everyone but has an unfair effect on people with the protected attribute (indirect discrimination).	• *SDA* • Other state and federal discrimination laws • *FWA* – unlawful termination and general protection provisions • WHS laws

Unlawful conduct	Definition	Relevant laws
Sex-based harassment	Any unwelcome conduct of a demeaning nature by reason of the person's sex in circumstances in which a reasonable person would have anticipated the possibility that the person harassed would be offended, humiliated or intimidated.	• *SDA* • State discrimination laws • WHS laws
Sexual harassment	Unwelcome sexual advance, or an unwelcome request for sexual favours, to the person harassed; or engages in other unwelcome conduct of a sexual nature in relation to the person harassed in circumstances in which a reasonable person, having regard to all the circumstances, would have anticipated the possibility that the person harassed would be offended, humiliated or intimidated.	• *SDA* • *FWA* – prohibition and applications for orders to stop sexual harassment • State discrimination laws • WHS laws
Conduct that creates a workplace that is hostile on the ground of sex	Workplace environments may be hostile (that is, offensive, intimidating or humiliating) to people of a particular sex, even if behaviour is not specifically directed at them or any person. This is because general actions can contribute to a workplace culture that makes people feel degraded, humiliated or offended in ways that are associated with their sex.	• *SDA* • WHS laws

Certain types of unlawful conduct may also be an offence under criminal law – for example, sexual assault, indecent assault, indecent exposure, stalking, obscene communications and recklessly or seriously causing injury.

There are many forms of unlawful contact, discrimination and harassment that this book does not have the bandwidth to cover. I do not intend to diminish the effects of those forms of discrimination on humans and our communities. A particular focus throughout the book is the gendered nature of discrimination, harassment and victimisation and the intersectional incidence and impact of this unlawful conduct.

Your WHS obligations

Obligations under WHS laws extend to ensuring the health of workers and that the conditions at the workplace are monitored to prevent illness or injury. This is particularly the case with the increased focus by regulators on psychosocial hazards in the workplace following the *Safe Work Australia Model Code of Practice: Managing psychosocial hazards at work*, which is being rolled out across Australia.[4]

In addition to the unlawful conduct defined earlier in this chapter, abuse and harassment directed at workers by customers can also pose reasonably foreseeable risks to workers' health, safety and welfare. As a leader you must take action to mitigate these risks.

Workers can apply for stop-bullying or sexual harassment orders if they are exposed to unlawful bullying and sexual harassment by third parties in the workplace and there is a risk that, unless orders are made, the unlawful conduct will continue.

'Work' is not confined to behaviour that occurs within the physical workplace but can encompass a worker's participation in activities authorised by the organisation, regardless of their location. Although you cannot completely control the behaviour of customers and third parties, you must take reasonable steps to shield your people from abuse. This may include creating charters or codes of conduct with customers and third parties to outline expectations of behaviours. You should also have policies in place for dealing with online harassment and situations where corporate social media accounts are used as vehicles by customers or others to make harassing, threatening or discriminatory posts about workers.

As social media continues to blur the lines between work and private life, what constitutes work activities as opposed to out-of-hours conduct becomes more difficult to decipher. The courts are more willing to broadly interpret the connection with employment if cyber bullying can be shown to be related to the victim-survivor's work or impact on their health, safety and welfare in the workplace.

As a leader you should ensure that a social media policy is in place which refers to cyber bullying and responsible use of the internet and social media, and that references the relationship between work and home. The policy should clearly outline what conduct amounts to a breach of the policy and the extent to which an employee's private social media posts can result in disciplinary action. It should include specific examples. As with other forms of poor behaviour, encouraging people to report incidents to leaders or HR departments is also essential. Bullying or harassment via social media will be harder for you to detect, and your ability to deal with any issues relies heavily on people coming forward with their concerns. For this reason, bullying and harassment training should reference conduct online to raise awareness and promote reporting.

This is more critical now in the wake of the positive duty to prevent discrimination, sexual harassment, sex-based harassment and conduct that creates sexually hostile workplaces in Australia. Taking all the appropriate steps to eliminate, as far as possible, unlawful conduct will promote a fair and supportive culture and mitigate significant risks to the organisation and serious harm to workers. This has never been more necessary.

A call for leadership

A survey commissioned by national violence prevention organisation, Our Watch, of 200 Australian business leaders revealed that up to 90 per cent of leaders believe sexual harassment at work is a serious issue and should be a priority for employers to address.[5]

In launching a Federal Government-funded national campaign to ensure employers adequately discharge their positive duty in the Respect@Work laws, Federal Assistant Minister for the Prevention of Family Violence, Justine Elliot said:

We have come too far as a society to continue to allow thousands of women to be pushed out of jobs and opportunities, as a consequence of employers not demonstrating the leadership required to ensure their safety and security. [6]

In a joint press release launching the campaign, Our Watch Chief Executive Officer Patty Kinnersly focused on the systemic drivers of sexual harassment we will discuss in this book, including sexism and disrespect, and the culture change that is required in Australian workplaces to create cultures of respect and equality. She noted:

Even a small increase in women in leadership roles results in reports of sexual harassment declining by more than 20 per cent in the years that follow. This is because these employers are more likely to have more policies that support gender equality in the workplace.[7]

The campaign emphasises that gender equality is of course not only about reducing sexual harassment and associated risks (what I call the fear factor) but also results in increased productivity, efficiency, innovation, creativity and employee engagement (what I call the benefit factor).[8]

To achieve safe and respectful workplaces we need leaders focused on both the fear and benefit factors. The emphasis should be that achieving gender equality and respect at work is win-win.

The media's role

One undeniable catalyst for change has been the media. It has played a significant role in movements such as #MeToo and #TimesUp in calling out these behaviours at work and, more to the point, the failure of leaders and boards to act on them. Transparency builds accountability which leads to change and general deterrence. The boards and leaders I talk to are highly motivated to avoid their organisation being the next in line. Now, more than ever, I am seeing an appetite to act on unacceptable behaviour rather than tolerating jerks at work.

Not a day passes without a cultural issue playing out in the media. The media fuels social media, and social media fuels the media. For the leaders addressing these issues, a vicious cycle ensues. The media, and indeed the court of public opinion, seems particularly interested in high-profile sexual harassment cases; corruption scandals; humans 'gone wild' featuring drug or alcohol abuse, altercations or other misconduct; and the systemic effect of bullying or discriminatory cultures. Supply chains are also increasingly coming under scrutiny, with organisations tainted by the failings of their subcontractors, franchisees or even suppliers. The bigger and more established the business or personal brands involved, the bigger the scandal.

There was a time when the boundaries between work and home were very clear. It was clear where work ended, and home life began. When humans did dumb things that got them fired, they did not necessarily have to confess their sins to family, friends or acquaintances or explain away their indiscretions to future employers. It's fair to say those days are gone.

In the modern world, transparency has increased, indiscretions and cultural issues are highly visible and scrutiny by the court of public opinion via online platforms and the media has reached new heights.

There is nowhere to hide. Breaches impact not only people's work lives and reputations but also their family lives and social relationships. Even if the story diffuses in a day or two, the online footprint is often indefinite and damming.

Cries for 'heads on a platter' often come before the organisation has even had an opportunity to investigate alleged misconduct. This often leaves leaders in a vulnerable position, trying to reconcile procedural fairness requirements with the health, safety and welfare of the humans they are responsible for (who are often distressed by the public scrutiny and online trolling), while simultaneously addressing the media to appease the public that they are taking matters seriously and will not tolerate unacceptable conduct.

The burden on leaders is particularly onerous given the known extent and effect of trolling on individuals psychologically, with tragically fatal consequences known to arise from such trolling in recent times.

So, when the court of public opinion next demands 'heads on a platter', answer back swiftly and succinctly to indicate the matter is in hand and that you will not tolerate the intolerable. Then pause and address the other critical steps necessary to protect your organisation by considering procedural requirements, including investigation and disciplinary procedures and the health, safety and welfare of all humans including the 'accused'. Offer access to employee assistance programs or other urgent counselling and support services.

The reality is that the media cycle will run its course regardless of what you say or do. The legacy of non-compliance in that period can however haunt you for months or years in a legal claim – or worse if the person is adversely or catastrophically affected by online trolling.

In my interview with Catherine Fox for this book, I asked her about the role the media has played in calling out toxic behaviour in the workplace and the failures of leaders and boards to act on it. Fox agreed the media has played a crucial role in shaping the narrative around these challenges, particularly through consumer-facing content.

She recalled pivotal moments that marked a shift in the discourse. Fox said there has been a public outcry about the lack of women on listed company boards, leading to some outspoken figures condemning the situation. Yet, the subsequent progress was gradual until the advent of the #MeToo movement.

Fox says while progress has been made, particularly with the rise of movements such as #MeToo, challenges persist, and the focus is still often on fixing women rather than challenging the bias in our workplace structures – which are mostly run by men. The media has played a vital role in covering these issues, with data becoming an essential tool in driving conversations forward. However, there is a concerning assumption prevalent in society that gender equity has been achieved, with almost 60 per cent of Australians believing we are close to reaching or have reached that goal.[9] This assumption can lead to complacency and reinforces inertia, hindering further progress. Despite positive strides in political representation and management positions, power is still overwhelmingly in the hands of men and there is a need to challenge their prevailing attitudes, beliefs and assumptions.

Fox concluded that while there have been positive steps towards addressing unlawful and toxic behaviour in the workplace, when it comes to the root cause of gender equality, there is still significant work to be done. The media has a responsibility to continue shedding light on these issues, utilising data and diverse perspectives to drive meaningful change and challenging current power dynamics. It is imperative to call out biased assumptions about who should be the boss, and strive for more inclusive leadership to create a truly equitable future.

Key actions

Bullying and sexual harassment are serious WHS risks with significant consequences for your business.

○ **ASSESS RISK FACTORS** for unlawful conduct in your workplace and take reasonably practicable steps to protect workers and measures to eliminate unlawful conduct.

○ **PROTECT WORKERS** from others' conduct, including customers and third parties at work and online.

○ **INVESTIGATE ALLEGATIONS** of unlawful conduct and follow person-centred, trauma-informed practices and procedurally fair investigation and disciplinary processes prior to termination of employment. (More guidance will be provided on this later in the book.)

○ **ENCOURAGE BYSTANDER ACTION** against unlawful conduct and act when they speak up.

○ **SHIFT THE FOCUS** to gender equality and building cultures that are safe, respectful and inclusive. Focus not only on risk minimisation but the benefits of doing so.

○ **DON'T TOLERATE UNLAWFUL CONDUCT** on your watch. Doing so will result in significant legal risks and exposure for your organisation and you personally, and damage to your organisation's brand, culture and performance and your reputation as a leader or HR professional.

Chapter 2

Riddled with fear

A fear-based workplace is one where fear, not trust, is the driving force. Trust and fear cannot co-exist; it is one or the other. In a fear-based workplace, everyone is focused on self-preservation: ensuring their own needs, deadlines and goals are met. People must self-protect in this environment because, if they fall short, their job is at risk. This negatively affects the culture, morale and mental health of everyone in the workplace and precludes problem-solving, solutions, innovation and collective performance.[10] Fear is like cancer in the workplace. It permeates and spreads, destroying the healthy behaviours that help humans trust, connect and thrive.

Fear is an intense negative emotion in response to a real or perceived danger or threat which invokes a fight, flight or freeze reaction. The impact of fear on psychological and physical health and safety is well documented.

Endocrinologist Dr Hans Selye identified three phases the human body goes through in response to stress, as summarised in Figure 3.[11]

FIGURE 3: THE BODY'S RESPONSE TO STRESS

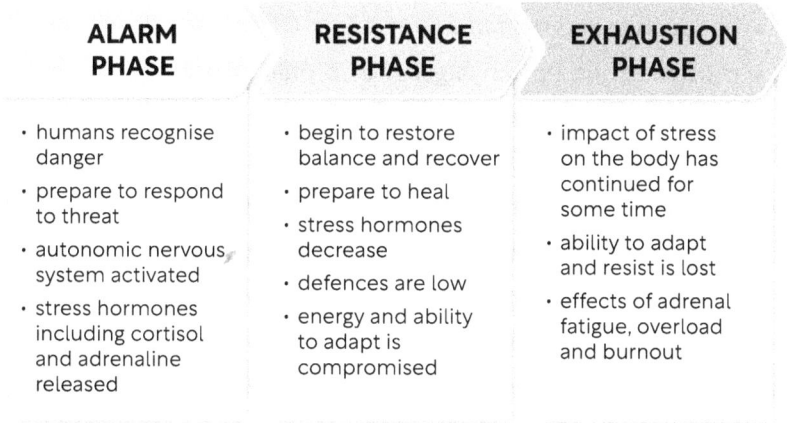

ALARM PHASE	RESISTANCE PHASE	EXHAUSTION PHASE
• humans recognise danger • prepare to respond to threat • autonomic nervous system activated • stress hormones including cortisol and adrenaline released	• begin to restore balance and recover • prepare to heal • stress hormones decrease • defences are low • energy and ability to adapt is compromised	• impact of stress on the body has continued for some time • ability to adapt and resist is lost • effects of adrenal fatigue, overload and burnout

It is important to recognise that while fear is a state of mind, it triggers a strong physical reaction in the human body. As soon as humans sense danger, our amygdala is activated and alerts our nervous system to release stress hormones. As a result our blood pressure and heart rate increase. Breathing intensifies. Blood flow changes, pulling away from the heart and into the limbs (to make it easier for us to throw punches as barbarians would or to run for our lives).[12]

While you may know conditions such as anxiety, depression, post-traumatic stress disorder and other mental health disturbances can result from fear, you may not realise chronic fear also significantly impacts physical health, with reports confirming the following (without limitation):

- immune system dysfunction
- endocrine system dysfunction
- autonomic nervous system alterations
- sleep disturbances
- eating disorders
- headaches and migraines
- muscle aches, fibromyalgia and chronic pain
- asthma and respiratory effects.[13]

I have laboured this point as it is very important for leaders to understand that, when we talk of psychosocial hazards throughout this book, we are not talking about touchy-feely nice-to-have stuff with insignificant consequences. The damage that can be caused by these hazards is serious and can be catastrophic, as is the risk of failing to address them.

Power

Power relates to the possession of control, authority or influence over others and has many dimensions. Power and gender inequality play a systemic role in perpetuating unlawful conduct and psychosocial hazards.

The *Respect@Work* website explains that the concept of power – specifically, the misuse of power – is central to understanding the causes of sexual harassment.[14] In the workplace, power is commonly thought to be associated with an individual's gender, seniority, age or value to a business. A harasser might be in a position of power due to being the owner of a business, a valued customer of a business, a direct supervisor of a person harassed, or in a position to influence that person's future career prospects.[15]

To prevent sexual harassment in the workplace, leaders are encouraged to understand the key underlying drivers of sexual harassment as a social problem. Stopping it is not just about altering the behaviour of individuals; we need to change the culture and environment of workplaces in which it occurs. To prevent sexual harassment from happening in the first place, we must recognise the systemic and contextual issues that drive these behaviours. Primary prevention is all about addressing the root causes (or drivers) of sexual harassment.[16]

The drivers of sexual harassment that as a leader you must address include:

- gender inequality
- power imbalances
- lack of accountability for prevention at senior levels
- specific industry or workplace factors such as poor workplace culture or inconsistent standards
- lack of demonstrated commitment to diversity and inclusion.[17]

Power blinds humans to others' perspectives. Research has revealed powerful people feel less distressed than others when someone sitting across from them tells a story of great personal hardship. They are also less likely to realise that others do not share their same privilege. A study of 500 participants found powerful people are likely to take cynical views of others' motivations, including about how they react to sexual harassment allegation. The researchers observed that, in workplaces:

cynicism from leadership regarding sexual misconduct can lead to what clinical psychologists refer to as 'institutional betrayal' – where the trauma of an assault is compounded by bureaucratic incompetence or opposition or indifference from management.[18]

The opposite of this is institutional courage, the researchers say, where victims are believed and bureaucracy is minimised.

Another study provided insights into the minds of those who perpetrate inappropriate workplace behaviours, including bullying at work.[19] It found that the reasons people bully are complex. It can be an interplay of factors, including the bullying individual wanting to have some form of power over others. Bullying can also stem from systemic issues such as gender bias, racism, jealousy or competitiveness, and a sense of elevated status. The study found bullying to be most prevalent among blue-collar and unskilled workers, and among men aged 25 to 34 without a university degree.[20]

The impact of bullying leaves victim-survivors struggling with poor self-esteem, anxiety and depression. As a result, absenteeism and turnover increase, and organisational productivity and performance can be negatively impacted. Leading humans is likened to nurturing plants. If all the right conditions are applied, they grow and flourish.[21]

Blame and criticism

Humans are naturally wired to blame other people or circumstances when things go wrong. The most destructive behaviours in relationships are criticism, contempt, defensiveness and stone-walling. These behaviours lead humans and teams down a negative spiral. Our brains interpret blame in the same way they interpret a physical attack.[22] When we are blamed, our prefrontal cortex effectively shuts down and directs all our energy to defence, which, ironically, sabotages our ability to solve the problem for which we are being blamed.[23]

In blame cultures, humans work under a cloud of fear and suspicion. Trust fades, resentment builds, compassion is lost and while everyone is looking after themselves, collective wisdom, growth, learning and performance is lost.[24] Short-termism destroys any long-term benefits that could otherwise be achieved by the efforts of the relentless individuals spinning their wheels and getting nowhere.

It's common in environments riddled with fear for leaders to focus on the weaknesses of humans in their teams and spend excessive time and energy criticising them. When leaders blame people for their weaknesses, this damages their confidence and detracts from their strengths and the benefits they bring.

I have long advocated for a focus on strengths rather than weaknesses in the workplace. This approach not only increases morale, confidence and motivation but it reduces fear, blame and burnout. It creates a workplace of more well-adjusted, thriving humans and significantly improves team and organisational performance.

These observations were validated by Gallup research which found that to improve performance, leaders should focus on people's strengths, not their weaknesses.[25] Traditional workplace development focuses on finding and fixing people's weaknesses. This results in a negative employee experience, mediocre performance improvements and humans who are less engaged.

Instead, developing strengths helps people become more confident, productive and self-aware. It leads to:

- 7 to 23 per cent higher employee engagement
- 8 to 18 per cent increase in performance
- 20 to 73 per cent lower attrition.[26]

This is something that, as leaders, we cannot lose sight of in building teams and developing humans. It's not a new phenomenon. As far back as the 1960s, Peter Drucker highlighted the need for focusing on strengths to get the best out of humans. He wrote: 'Focusing on strengths is development, whereas focusing on weakness is damage control [leading to] misuse, if not abuse of the person.'

Of course, we cannot be all things to all people. Everyone has weaknesses. No-one is a perfect all-rounder. Humans are all made up of an imperfect mix of unique strengths and weaknesses. While weaknesses cannot be completely ignored, you can build teams with complementary skills, focus on the strengths each person brings and harness the fruits of their collective labour, wisdom and insights. That is what makes you a good leader.

Psychological safety

Psychological safety is the shared belief that it is safe to speak out, take risks and learn alongside each other. It invokes a willingness to be candid and vulnerable with each other, and the belief that doing so will be valued, respected and reciprocated, rather than punished.[27]

Brain imaging experiments have demonstrated that increased oxytocin results in a reduction in fear and enhances psychological safety. The more oxytocin the human brain makes, the more the person feels empathy and connection with others and is willing to help, collaborate and support. Conversely, when humans view others as different, psychological safety is diminished, and team performance is adversely affected.[28] This research is part of the foundation of how you can establish trust and psychological safety at work, which we will explore further in Part II.

Brené Brown, in her work on vulnerability in leadership, provides leading guidance on this. While vulnerability is important for everyone, it is critical for leaders, particularly when they are struggling to be authentic in the conversations they have with humans in their organisations. Brown says being vulnerable creates a space for leaders to let others into their heads. As a leader, it is important to remember that humans in your workplace know if something is not working or right. They want you to have the courage to tell them so you can work together towards a solution.

Key actions

Fear and blame destroy trust. Trust is necessary for a safe and inclusive workplace.

○ **RECOGNISE FEAR** as serious WHS risk with potentially catastrophic consequences of the health and safety of your people.

○ **THE ANTITHESIS OF FEAR IS TRUST.** As trust and fear cannot co-exist in the workplace, to combat the negative impacts of fear, leaders should focus on building trust by:
   - showing vulnerability
   - fostering and encouraging a growth mindset that reinforces learning from mistakes
   - focusing on strengths rather than weaknesses of people in their team.

Chapter 3

On the verge of burnout

The term 'burnout' originated in the 1970s but the reality no doubt existed long before then. Burnout is an extreme state of stress, leading to emotional, mental and physical exhaustion. It is more than ordinary fatigue and makes it difficult to handle daily tasks and responsibilities. Humans suffering from burnout often feel they have nothing left to give and no purpose. When left untreated, burnout can develop into serious physical and mental health conditions.

According to Mental Health First Aid Australia, a recent study indicated Australian workers reported among the highest burnout rates in the world. An alarming 61 per cent of respondents reported experiencing burnout, compared to the global average of 48 per cent. This represented a 5 per cent increase in burnout reported by Australian workers in 2022 alone, and burnout was said to have been attributed to 40 per cent of resignations. Burnout and stress-related absenteeism was reported as costing the Australian economy an estimated $14 billion every year.[29]

According to ReachOut Australia, common signs of burnout include:

- feeling exhausted and unable to perform basic tasks
- losing motivation in many aspects of your life, including your work, hobbies or relationships
- feeling unable to focus or concentrate on tasks
- feeling empty or lacking in emotion
- losing your passion and drive
- being easily irritated by small problems
- experiencing conflict in your relationships with co-workers, friends and family
- emotionally withdrawing from friends and family.[30]

In a systemic review of the physical, psychological and occupational consequences of burnout, it was established that work demands such as high workload and time pressure led to negative outcomes and burnout. Conversely work resources such as autonomy, peer support and engagement were found to contribute to positive outcomes that are described as motivational processes. It was established that leadership had a direct effect on the investigated outcomes which included employability, performance and commitment and an indirect effect on burnout and engagement by reducing demands and increasing job resources.[31]

The study confirmed the physical and psychological consequences, only some of which include:

- Physical consequences:
  - obesity
  - type 2 diabetes
  - cholesterol
  - heart disease
  - chronic pain
  - fatigue
  - headaches
  - respiratory infections
  - gastrointestinal problems
  - respiratory infections
  - mortality below 45

- Psychological consequences:
  - insomnia
  - depressive symptoms
  - psychotropic and antidepressive treatment
  - hospitalisation for mental disorders
  - psychological ill-health symptoms.[32]

When Stanford researchers investigated how workplace stress affects health costs and mortality in the United States, they found that it led to spending of nearly US$190 billion – roughly 8 per cent of national healthcare outlays – and nearly 120,000 deaths each year.[33]

Worldwide, 615 million suffer from depression and anxiety and, according to a recent World Health Organization (WHO) study and costs the global workforce an estimated US$1 trillion in lost productivity each year.[34]

According to a 2023 report by the Leaders Lab:

- 69 per cent of leaders are burned out
- 54 per cent of team members are burned out
- 91 per cent of leaders have been feeling burned out for 'some time' or longer.[35]

A Gallup survey of 7500 full-time workers listed the top five reasons for burnout, which are shown in Figure 4.

FIGURE 4: THE TOP FIVE REASONS FOR BURNOUT

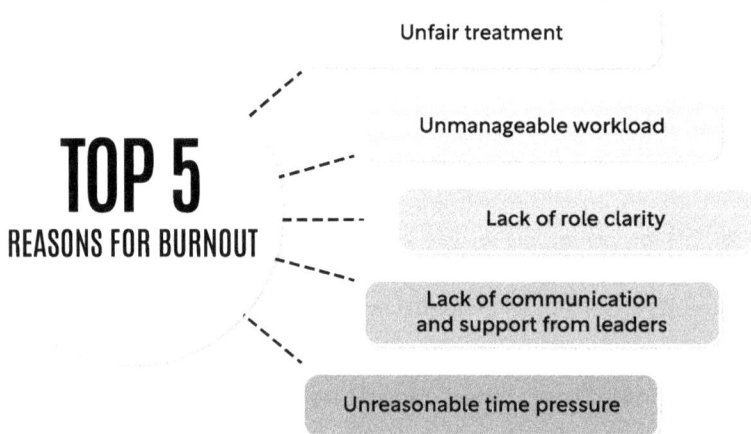

TOP 5
REASONS FOR BURNOUT

- Unfair treatment
- Unmanageable workload
- Lack of role clarity
- Lack of communication and support from leaders
- Unreasonable time pressure

Adapted from Wigert and Agrawal 2018[36]

To add to this, carers face further pressures as they feel overwhelmed and exhausted by the daily demands of raising a family. Often, before our children are independent as they study and stay home for longer, we're also caring for ageing and elderly relatives who are living longer. Juggling the countless responsibilities of care, home maintenance and work can take its toll, leading to intense fatigue and a deterioration of physical and mental health. I have repeatedly said the struggle is in the juggle and the struggle is real.

Mental health in the workplace

The increased incidence of workplace mental health issues is undeniable, and it's a minefield for organisations and leaders to navigate. It's unclear whether the spike in workplace mental health issues arises from an increase in diagnoses, preparedness of employees to discuss these issues, or, indeed, an increased incidence because of constant connectivity and work 'creep'. Regardless, it can be hard for leaders and HR professionals to know how to handle these cases. We have seen many education campaigns and programs focused on improving workplace mental health and wellbeing, yet things do not seem to be improving, and the minefield of obligations leaders are navigating often feels irreconcilable.

Even where a person's condition is not caused by their employment, leaders are walking a tightrope to ensure the worker performs the inherent requirements of the role (often with reasonable adjustments as required by law to enable them to safely do so) while:

- protecting their health and safety and that of others in the workplace
- not discriminating against them based on protected attributes under state and federal discrimination laws
- not unlawfully terminating or taking 'adverse action' against them based on protected attributes in breach of the *FWA*

- not unfairly dismissing them in a manner that is harsh, unjust or unreasonable under the *FWA*.

At the time of writing this book, the High Court of Australia has granted special leave to appeal a ruling that an employer could not have reasonably foreseen an extraordinary psychiatric response to an employee who was dismissed for an altercation with a hotel owner while on a work trip. It has been an interesting matter to follow. There is a broad principle that, as leaders, we take people as we find them and should ensure their health and safety while in the workplace. The question is: how far does this principle go? Should leaders be responsible for an extraordinary and unforeseen response by an employee to what is otherwise reasonable management action taken in a reasonable manner? This case will provide some guidance on this point, although the employer has fallen short of managing a procedure beyond reproach by in this case, failing to follow its own disciplinary procedures.

The High Court will consider whether:

1. the employer had a non-delegable duty of care to its employees to take reasonable care to avoid exposing them to unnecessary risks of injury

2. the employer's duty of care and consequent exposure to damages extends to providing 'safe' disciplinary and dismissal processes that protect sacked workers from psychiatric injury.

In the application for special leave, the worker submitted 'the employment relationship is in certain respects uniquely personal – including in many cases indicating vulnerability – underscores the basis for recoverability'.

Where leaders and HR professionals are on notice of a pre-existing mental health condition or risk of self-harm by an employee during a disciplinary process or following the termination of employment, even if on valid grounds, the stakes are high. These are difficult matters to manage and are ones we recommend you seek legal advice and the support of a trained health professional to work through. While there may still be a question to be determined on how far an employer's duty goes in these cases, as leaders and HR professionals you should take all steps to ensure humans are safe at work and as they leave your care in the workplace.

When leaders burn out

Leaders themselves are also increasingly burning out. According to an article published in *Harvard Business Review*, this is sometimes due to the trend towards servant leadership – something I have observed in practice.[37] Flatter structures and cultural change in leadership styles has brought us more compassionate, human-centred workplaces, but has also led to leader burnout.

The notion humans are in a role to serve others makes it very hard to say one word – a word that I personally attest to finding challenging to say: *no*. Those two little letters often feel impossible to muster up. In servant leadership, leaders and their people are reactive, trying to please everyone. This often leads to pleasing no-one, and everyone burning out.

Instead of servant leadership, leaders are encouraged to shift towards what is described as 'noble-purpose leadership'.[38] This is when leaders and their people are in shared pursuit of a cause bigger than themselves (their team, their customers, their community) and their goal is to positively impact their constituents rather than serving them.[39]

The same *Harvard Business Review* article states that, in noble-purpose leadership, leaders can create a subtle yet powerful shift by calibrating to a higher purpose.[40] They can ask questions such as: what do *you* need to be successful in accomplishing our goal? What help will *you* need? This reframes the emotional dynamic. Instead of the leader having to be solely responsible for supporting the team member, asking what they need to be successful creates a shared sense of responsibility. The leader is purposefully positioning them-selves to have a positive impact on the person's results, yet they are not taking on sole responsibility for supporting them.[41]

As this book was being completed, the *FWA* was amended to include a new right to disconnect for employees across Australia. While many leaders called me in a panic when the laws were announced, fearful they would not be able to contact staff out of hours, this is not in fact what the law says. Although you should be circumspect in contact given the underlying psychosocial hazard this could be under WHS laws, the right employees have under the FWA is to 'refuse to monitor, read or respond to contact, or attempted contact' from their employer (or related parties) outside their work hours, unless it's unreasonable to do so.

There is a non-exhaustive list of factors that must be considered in determining whether a refusal is unreasonable, including:

- the reason for the contact or attempted contact
- how the contact or attempted contact is made and the level of disruption the contact or attempted contact causes the employee
- the extent to which the employee is compensated (which includes non-monetary compensation):
  - to remain available to perform work during the period in which the contact or attempted contact is made, or
  - for working additional hours outside of the employee's ordinary hours of work
- the nature of the employee's role and the employee's level of responsibility
- the employee's personal circumstances (including family or caring responsibilities)
- whether the contact is required under a law of the Commonwealth, state or territory.

Naturally, employees and leaders may have different opinions on what constitutes 'reasonable contact'. To address this, there will be a process for dispute resolution, which involves taking disagreements to the Fair Work Commission. Before doing so the employee and employer must try to resolve the dispute at their workplace. If these discussions don't resolve the issue, employees can approach the Commission to make a 'stop order' and/or otherwise deal with the dispute.

I raise this here as I have observed that the more leaders are required to ensure the health, safety and wellbeing of humans working with them including by respecting their right to disconnect, the more leaders carry the load and risk of burnout. The operational pressure, organisational risk and legal burden on leaders has never been so high.

It is critical that organisations recognise this and adopt strategies to ensure leaders have sufficient support in the workplace, adequate respite, breaks and access to professional health services and coaching support as required to ensure their health and safety. They are our frontline and human fire wall when it comes to both operations and risk. We cannot afford for them to fall over.

Burnout is not a badge of honour

Ryan McGrory is the founder of Exsona.[42] For over a decade, he has been designing successful strategies and developing impactful programs to improve workplace culture. In an interview for this book, he said:

> Burnout can lead to death. We do not really acknowledge this. We sort of treat burnout as this badge of honour, sometimes – as if it is something to be admired – and we often downplay its impact.

Burnout is not just about being tired, McGrory said. It can have severe physical and mental health consequences, including chronic stress, anxiety, depression and physical ailments such as cardiovascular issues. For an organisation, worker burnout causes decreased productivity and engagement, negative team dynamics and increased turnover.

Leaders in the workplace are responsible for preventing burnout – they should have plans, controls and solutions in place to reduce or eliminate the stressors that can lead to burnout. According to McGrory:

> [The entire 'wellbeing' response has been] to introduce an employee assistance program – which, really, is a crisis-response solution when things are already in a bad spot – or workplace wellness programs, which are often about yoga, mindfulness and fruit bowls … all great things, but none of it really prevents burnout.

McGrory points out that the wellbeing challenges and problems within each organisation are typically quite unique – they differ depending on the demographics, industry and culture. There is rarely a one-size-fits-all approach. What we know works is the process of developing a wellbeing and mental health strategy that focuses on researching the workplace; providing solutions that promote positive practices that improve health; reducing risks by identifying psychosocial hazards and managing or removing them; and supporting those who need support to return to optimum health as soon as possible.

Key actions

Burnout breaks humans in your workplace, impacting their health and safety, increasing risk and damaging workplace culture and organisational performance.

○ **RECOGNISE THE SIGNIFICANT HARM** burnout can cause and treat is as a serious WHS risk that can result in significant liability for the organisation and its leaders.

○ **ASSESS THE SYSTEMIC AND CULTURAL DRIVERS** of burnout, identify specific drivers and risk factors in your workplace (e.g. workload, work design and relationships at work) and introduce measures to address and manage these risks.

○ **ALWAYS ENSURE THE HEALTH AND SAFETY OF HUMANS** including on their way out the door by adopting safe disciplinary procedures that consider the impact on their personal health and safety in light of known vulnerabilities and health conditions they have disclosed.

○ **DON'T FORGET TO LOOK AFTER YOURSELVES** and each other as HR professionals and leaders!

Chapter 4

Killer cultures

Despite nationwide education campaigns and protective juris-dictions in Australia designed to 'stop the bullying', and criminal consequences for breach of WHS laws, the incidence of bullying and mental health claims in Australian workplaces is increasing. It is however possible the decreased stigma around mental health conditions and increased awareness and encouragement to talk about them has been a factor in the increase in reporting.

According to the Australian Bureau of Statistics National Study of Mental Health and Wellbeing released in 2023, 42.9 per cent of Australians have experienced a mental health condition at some point in their life. Alarmingly, one in six Australians (16.7 per cent or 3.3 million people) aged 16 to 85 years had experienced suicidal thoughts or behaviours in their life with 3.3 per cent (644,600 people) having experienced suicidal thoughts or behaviours in the previous 12 months.[43]

Many of the matters we now work on in our practice include allegations of psychosocial hazards and the harm arising from them. Emerging data from insurers and regulators supports the increased incidence of these claims. As the incidence of mental health in the community increases, so does its manifestation – and the consequences on humans in the workplace resulting from psychosocial hazards, including toxic and fear-inducing conduct, the expectation of excessive work hours and pressures leading to burnout.

Safe Work Australia identifies psychosocial hazards as hazards that may cause psychological harm (whether or not they may also cause physical harm). People who are exposed to psychosocial hazards at work are at greater risk of developing a work-related psychological injury, and experience poorer mental health outcomes. Mental health conditions are an increasing proportion of work-related injuries and illnesses in Australia. In 2021–22, mental health conditions accounted for 9 per cent (11,700) of all serious claims and 7 per cent of all work-related injuries and illnesses. This represented a 36.9 per cent increase in claims since 2017–18, compared to an increase of 18.3 per cent for all serious claims over the period.[44]

The *Safe Work Australia Model Code of Practice: Managing psychosocial hazards at work* also emphasises that psychosocial hazards can cause psychological and physical harm and confirms that, on average, work-related psychological injuries have longer recovery times, higher costs, and require more time away from work than physical injuries.[45] It follows that managing the risks associated with psychosocial hazards decreases the disruption associated with staff turnover and absenteeism and may improve broader organisational performance and productivity.[46]

Further, reports have for some time confirmed the significant gains for organisations in creating psychologically healthy workplaces where it is perceived that leaders have made workers' health and wellbeing a priority. Safe Work Australia found that initiatives to create psychologically healthy workplaces return $2.30 for every $1 spent.[47]

Toxic workplace culture contributed to suicide

In October 2023, an independent statutory body pleaded guilty to a criminal charge under Victorian WHS laws for failing to provide and maintain a safe workplace.

The WorkSafe Victoria press release referred to the statutory body being 'convicted and fined $379,157 over a toxic workplace culture … that contributed to the suicide of one worker and numerous others taking stress leave'.[48]

These are words we, as leaders and HR professionals, never want to read.

The cause of the 'toxic culture' was seemingly compounding, with the regulator reporting that over a period of nearly three years, risks arose from:

- exposure to traumatic materials
- role conflict
- high workloads and work demands

- poor workplace relationships and inappropriate workplace behaviours which resulted in numerous complaints regarding allegations including:
  - bullying
  - favouritism and cronyism
  - verbal abuse
  - derogatory comments
  - intimidation
  - invasions of privacy
  - perceived threats to future progression.[49]

As result of these reported psychosocial hazards, many workers took leave and were said to have reported the impacts of these hazards on them personally as anxiety, post-traumatic stress disorder, stress, fear and humiliation. Some did not return. One senior worker had three months off work with a major depressive disorder before tragically taking her own life.[50]

In entering a plea of guilty, the body admitted it failed to undertake appropriate risk assessments relating to the psychological health of its workers.[51]

At the conclusion of the matter, WorkSafe Executive Director of Health and Safety, Narelle Beer, said in a powerful statement:

Everyone in an organisation has a role to play in creating a healthy and safe environment, but the development of a positive culture and appropriate risk control measures depends on leadership from the top. It is an employer's legal duty to do everything they possibly can to support their workers to thrive in their roles and ensure they leave work each day no worse than how they arrived.

Employer failed to protect female workers from gendered violence in the workplace[52]

A youth care provider was recently fined $300,000 under NSW WHS laws and ordered to pay SafeWork's costs of $140,000 after it pleaded guilty to charges relating to its failures to protect the health and safety of two female care workers. The workers were diagnosed with PTSD after working at a home care facility for young people with high needs in South-Western Sydney.

The female workers were subjected to repeated threats of physical and sexual violence, sexual harassment, unwanted sexual touching and racism by three teenage residents with significant behavioural difficulties. The incidents included the worst kind of gendered expletives directed at the workers; one resident threatening a worker he would 'gut her like a pig' whilst holding a knife; threats of rape and physical violence including one resident motioning to slit a worker's throat; and a resident throwing a worker on a bed and jumping on top of her. The incident was not reported to police until a few months later, resulting in the resident being charged. After the resident was charged by police, the employer conducted risk assessments which confirmed the resident posed a very high risk to female workers.

In just four months there had been 33 occasions when a female worker was rostered alone on an overnight shift with the resident before he was charged by police despite the employer being aware he had previous assault charges for attacking women. There were discussions of rostering male workers only to the home but the area manager indicated she preferred not to in case they needed to move residents between houses. Further, the area manager was aware of incidents at the home and declined requests to attend the facility.

Justice Scotting who heard the matter in the NSW District Court held the employer failed to ensure the health and safety of the female workers finding that:

- The employer knew that each of the three youths eventually housed in the facility might engage in work-related violence and should have known there was a 'high risk of inappropriate sexual behaviour and aggression by the residents towards female workers'.
- There were multiple failures by management in responding to the risks and incidents and the area manager's response was 'seriously inadequate'.
- Undertaking risk assessments was an available step that would have caused little inconvenience to the employer given it already performed risk assessments for the benefit of residents. Extending this to consider the risk to the workers 'was not burdensome and would have identified the risk to female workers and that it could have been eliminated by removing female direct care workers from the home.'
- The risk of sexualised violence towards female workers could have been eliminated by engaging only male direct

care workers. The employer accepted it should have:

- conducted risk assessments regarding risks to workers *before* each resident moved in;
- in relation to one of the residents: (i) developed and implemented a behavioural support plan; (ii) engaged male direct care workers to work with him; and (iii) provided an after-hours response team.

Justice Scotting's ruling emphasised the employer's failure to prioritise the safety of its workers, highlighting the potential effectiveness of measures identified above which were deemed feasible and could have eliminated the risks of sexualised violence towards female workers.

While acknowledging the challenges in managing youth with behavioural issues noting the employer had 'very few means at its disposal to try to change the behaviour of the young persons' whilst also ensuring they were not deprived of their liberties and privileges, the judgment emphasised the employer's paramount responsibility to take proactive steps to ensure the health and safety of its workers.

Following this decision SafeWork called on organisations to regularly risk-assess workplace designs and environments that might contribute to violence and harassment, such as working at night, alone, in remote or isolated settings, directly with clients or at clients' home reiterating the need to address safety risks and take proactive, preventative action to ensure workers are protected from harm, including from violence and sexual harassment by third parties in the workplace.

Bullying and performance management

Safe Work Australia's *Guide for Preventing and Responding to Workplace Bullying* provides examples of what may be considered bullying if they are repeated, unreasonable and create a risk to health and safety.[53] Some of these are included in Figure 5.

FIGURE 5: EXAMPLES OF BULLYING BEHAVIOUR

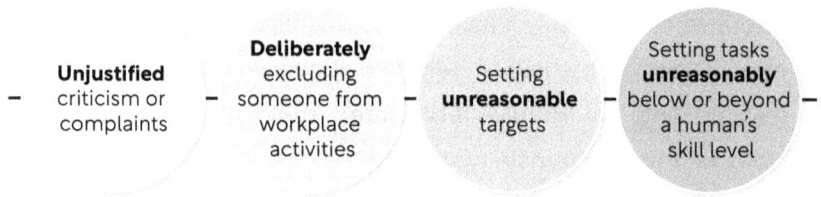

— **Unjustified** criticism or complaints — **Deliberately** excluding someone from workplace activities — Setting **unreasonable** targets — Setting tasks **unreasonably** below or beyond a human's skill level —

Adapted from Safe Work Australia 2016[54]

The words I've emphasised illustrate the fine line leaders must walk between exercising management prerogative and falling foul of these provisions. While performance management guidelines and disciplinary procedures are a great place to start to demonstrate the 'reasonableness' of actions taken, it is often the 'soft skills' used to implement these that will reduce the risk of complaint.

Situations often arise where people are hired or promoted, and it transpires that, despite their best efforts, activities and pursuits, they are just not cut out for the job. The challenge for leaders in these circumstances is 'calling it out' early and having conversations rather than letting the situation fester. Leaving these situations unaddressed causes increased frustration and reduced tolerance for leaders, and fear, insecurity and performance anxiety for the underperforming workers. This often escalates to absenteeism, claims and complaints where leaders are alleged to have crossed the 'reasonable management action' line. We can cynically say that some of these claims are made by workers to increase their protection and remedies if their employment is terminated, or to prevent the termination by increasing the legal risk stakes for employers and leaders. However there is also an evident impact from leaders failing to appropriately lead humans who are not working out to a fair and dignified exit with compassion and grace. This not only reduces harm to the affected worker but legal liability for the business and leader.

The challenge with systemic unaddressed underperformance is of course that boundaries blur: performance challenges can lead to absences and absences lead to further performance deficiencies. It is critical for leaders in these situations to separate the performance issues from the temporary absence from work, bullying or compensation claim as these are unlawful grounds to act upon in disciplining or terminating a person's employment.

As a leader it is necessary to have constructive and supportive conversations not only to provide people with a reasonable opportunity to improve and preserve their employment, but to minimise risks and exposures both the organisation and leader may face. While written records of performance discussions are important to demonstrate the process that has been followed (and indeed the reasonableness of it), these should only be compiled *after* a conversation with the person, allowing them an opportunity to respond, have their say, ask questions or request accommodations, resources, training or support.

I encourage everyone to adopt a growth mindset when managing performance or human error in the workplace. A growth mindset is based on the belief that a human's basic qualities are things they can cultivate through their efforts. Although people may differ in their innate talents, knowledge, skills, abilities or temperaments, everyone can change and grow through application and experience.[55]

Situations where someone is just not right for the job due to a bad hiring decision should be distinguished from when people make mistakes, unfortunate and catastrophic as they may be. Research undertaken by Dr Emma Seppälä provides helpful insights on this. While the traditional approach is to reprimand someone who has made a mistake, the more effective approach is to show compassion which in turn increases human loyalty and trust.[56] Importantly, the research shows:

> *Creating an environment where there is fear, anxiety and lack of trust makes humans shut down ... their threat response is engaged, their cognitive control is impacted. Consequently, their productivity and creativity diminish ... when trust, loyalty, and creativity are high, and stress is low, employees are happier and more productive, and turnover is lower.[57]*

Compassionate leaders understand that sometimes humans will win and sometimes they will learn.

Key actions

Psychosocial hazards are serious and pervasive WHS issues that can result in catastrophic consequences. To address them, you should:

○ **CONSULT WITH WORKERS** and **UNDERTAKE DETAILED RISK ASSESSMENTS FOR SPECIFIC HAZARDS** in your workplace including psychosocial hazards and the risk of aggression and violence by third parties in the workplace.

○ **PROACTIVELY AND CAREFULLY CONSIDER AND ASSESS RISKS** to workers vulnerable to aggression, violence or psychosocial harm including by third parties in the workplace including based on gender, age, race or other protected attributes or because of the working environment or nature of the role.

○ **DEVELOP CONTROL MEASURES AND TAKE PROACTIVE STEPS** to eliminate or minimise psychosocial hazards and other risks to worker health and safety, including from third parties in the workplace, as far as reasonably practicable.

○ **DEVELOP POLICIES AND PROCEDURES** that are tailored to your workplace to ensure compliance but sufficiently flexible to consider and manage your risks in specific circumstances as they arise.

○ **IMPLEMENT ANTI-BULLYING POLICIES AND PROCEDURES** ensuring workers and leaders are trained on them and understand the difference between bullying and reasonable management action.

○ **IMPLEMENT COMPLIANT PERFORMANCE MANAGEMENT** and **DISCIPLINARY PROCESSES** to manage employee conduct and performance at work by ensuring reasonable management action is undertaken in a reasonable manner.

○ **PRACTISE COMPASSIONATE LEADERSHIP** and encourage a growth mindset. If employees need to be exited, manage the process to ensure they leave with dignity.

Chapter 5

Escaping violence

According to previous Our Watch Ambassador Lucy Turnbull AO, 'violence against women is both a symptom and cause of gender inequality – and equality is at the heart of the solution.' In a powerful statement on the Our Watch website, she is reported as saying:

> For women to be safe, they must be equal. This is the story that needs to be told to end violence against women in this country. This issue is gendered. It's about power. It's about control. It's about exclusion. The evidence is clear. It robs on average a woman a week of their life, and it risks denying all women the right to reach their full potential. [58]

In 2023 alone, according to the Red Heart Campaign, 76 women were killed in Australia, many by a current or former intimate partner.[59] In some weeks towards a horrific end to the year, almost one woman was killed a day. As this book is being finalised, the Red Heart

Campaign has reported 35 women killed in Australia in just over five months in 2024. Sit with that for a moment. To quote Annabel Crabb: 'If a man got killed by a shark every week, we'd probably arrange for the ocean to be drained.'[60]

I am sick of counting dead women. They are mothers, daughters, sisters, friends, employees, colleagues, neighbours, humans – with lives, hopes and dreams and people who love them all. Women and their loved ones who are shattered when their lives are abruptly taken in a moment of rage, often when they try to leave. Why don't they leave? Because leaving is often deadly for women trying to escape an intimate partner, even in 'relationships' (if we call them that) as short as a few weeks.

We cannot stay silent on these issues. Communities, politicians, business leaders and all humans must speak up and act.

Full Stop is one of Australia's leading sexual, domestic and family violence response and recovery services that I gained harrowing insights from when serving as a Non Executive Director. According to Full Stop Australia CEO Karen Bevan:

> Prevention and response services are profoundly under-resourced. If we expect to end sexual, domestic and family violence in a generation (as per the National Plan), then more needs to be done ... We need a whole-of-community response to support women and children's safety ... We need this to be a genuine and sustained priority throughout all our systems – it means changing attitudes, directing resources and educating everyone about gender equality.

I'm past sad when I see the faces of these women in the media. I'm past disappointment and the other polite words we use to express sorrow. My blood bloody boils every time I hear another woman has been killed. My heart aches for the families including children who are left behind and the lives that are destroyed. What's more horrifying is that behind these faces of women who are tragically and horrifically killed are countless faceless women who are terrorised, tortured and coerced every day. At least 3600 women are admitted to hospital each year because of assault. Five thousand calls are placed to police about domestic and family violence (DFV) every week.[61]

As Holly Wainwright so powerfully said:

> The men who kill women do not look like monsters. They are not easy to pick out in a room. ... So many average monsters who look like your friend, your brother, your father, your boss, your boyfriend, your husband. And so many women ... Lost at the hands of such 'good blokes'. [62]

Devastatingly, demand for domestic violence services outweighs capacity to supply. What happens to those who are turned away, having fled their homes, potentially with their children? Where on earth do they go? What on earth do they do? This is unimaginable. Unfathomable. There really are no words to describe it. It simply shouldn't be.

Protecting victim-survivors at work

Leaders and workplaces play a critical role in ensuring they are protecting workers who may be subject to domestic violence. The statistics are such that these women *are* in our workplaces and our neighbourhoods. This problem is not isolated and discrete, it is widespread, indiscriminate and endemic. It is not out of sight and out of reach, it is happening in our own backyards, and we must open our eyes, hearts and minds to address it together.

A national Monash University study revealed the ways DFV profoundly impacts the working lives of victim-survivors.[63] It found that, of the 3002 victim-survivors surveyed, one in four reported that DFV significantly impacted their ability to undertake their job. Of the 2515 victim-survivors who reported that their job was impacted by their experience of DFV:

- One in two victim-survivors reported DFV negatively impacted their career progression and opportunities.
- Two in three victim-survivors reported DFV impacted their ability to concentrate at work.
- Two in five victim-survivors reported DFV impacted their productivity.
- Two in five victim-survivors reported DFV impacted their ability to enjoy their job.
- One in three victim-survivors reported DFV led them to socially withdraw from co-workers.
- One in three victim-survivors reported DFV negatively impacted their employment status.
- One in four victim-survivors reported DFV impacted their relationships at work.
- One in four victim-survivors reported DFV impacted their punctuality for work.

This research demonstrated that understanding the link between DFV and reduced work performance is essential to inform workplace support practice and policies, ensuring that victim-survivors are not subjected to performance management, at risk of demotion or employment termination.[64]

The Monash University study uncovered the alarming scope of perpetrator workplace interference in Australia, revealing that nearly 50 per cent of the survey respondents had experienced workplace interference strategies at some point during their experience of DFV. Concerningly, the study revealed that impeding access to employment is a key tactic utilised by DFV perpetrators:

> The data shows that abusers not only make it difficult for victim-survivors to engage in paid employment, but also tactically impede victim-survivors' abilities to perform, advance career goals and to thrive at work.[65]

Critically for leaders, the study found that one in five survey respondents worked in the same workplace as their abuser. Three in five of the victim-survivors who worked alongside their abuser reported that the abuser held a position of power above them in the workplace, with the authors cautioning:

> This is a particularly concerning finding because of the range of ways in which workplace hierarchies can further reinforce pre-existing power imbalances in relationships and facilitate further opportunities for abuse and control. These findings have important implications for employee safety, duty of care and the provision of supports.[66]

The authors of this study confirmed, with significant validated research and authority, what I have been witnessing and advising employers for years. To better support DFV victim-survivors, a shift in thinking is required whereby Australian workplaces and leaders recognise that DFV and work are entirely inseparable. DFV-informed understanding and assessment of work performance is essential and must be accompanied by a range of workplace supports designed to both support individual victim-survivors and to mitigate the impacts of victimisation on workforce participation. [67]

The Monash University study demonstrates the significant work that needs to be done to improve the response of organisations and leaders to DFV. Australian workplaces and leaders must prioritise the implementation of DFV workplace policies together with the cultivation of compassionate, trauma-informed workplace cultures. This includes workforce education to debunk myths and educate individuals on the phenomenon of DFV, recognising that 'workplaces have a vital role to play in supporting the safety and recovery needs of victim-survivors'.[68]

All employees in Australia are entitled to family or domestic violence leave. This leave extends beyond employees' existing sick and personal carers' leave entitlements, allowing all employees (including casuals) time off to go to the police, obtain legal advice, seek medical advice or arrange for new accommodation during work hours.

According to Safe Work Australia, organisations should provide a safe environment for workers to disclose family or domestic violence, assuring them of confidentiality and help in identifying risks.[69] Leaders and other workers may also notice signs of family and domestic violence, such as frequent unexplained bruising or injuries, excessive absence or lateness, inability to take work-related trips or receiving excessive personal calls or visits. Risks may change over time and leaders should continue to engage with workers on health and safety issues, particularly when workers are not physically co-located and risks are less evident — this is especially the case in workplaces where many people work from home.

Of course, organisations and leaders can help beyond the minimum legislative requirements to actively respond to domestic violence. This can include:

- taking a personalised and humane approach to implementing DFV leave policies by offering increased leave or broader entitlements and benefits to employees
- having nominated staff who are known to workers and trained in responding safely and in a trauma-informed manner
- offering all workers training on supports available for those experiencing family and domestic violence
- ensuring employees have access to confidential support within and external to the organisation to disclose family and domestic violence
- developing and implementing personalised safety plans for an emergency response to instances of family and domestic violence including when to involve police
- offering flexible work arrangements, such as adjustments to working hours or work locations
- providing short-term loans (such as for bond payments) or alternative short-term accommodation to employees who are fleeing violence.

A national emergency

One of the best books I have read in recent years is *See What You Made Me Do* by the phenomenal Walkley Award–winning journalist Jess Hill, which was turned into an SBS documentary series.[70] It is not an easy read, but it is a necessary one. It's necessary to understand the dangers of domestic abuse, which Hill says 'we ignore, explain away or refuse to see'. This equally applies in the workplace: its critical that leaders understand the warning signs that someone in their workplace may be experiencing the horrors of coercive control.

We often hear about the dangers of women walking on the street at night, but do you know where the most dangerous place for a woman is? In her own home.

Hill says domestic violence is not just a series of isolated incidents. It's the acts that lead to entrapment of a person that wear them down to the point where they lose the connection and support of the outside world and no longer recognise themselves. Actual violence is not always necessary for coercive control to exist, just the believable threat of violence, which is a form of torture in and of itself. Hill says:

> *Domestic abuse is a national emergency: one in four women has experienced violence from a man she was intimate with. But too often we ask only one question: why didn't she leave? We should be asking: why did he do it?*

As a leader you can and should also take disciplinary action against abusers if they are using workplace resources such as work time, phones, email and computer systems to threaten, harass or abuse and consider whether matters should be reported to the police.

When I asked Catherine Fox about the role of employers in addressing this crisis in the workplace, she referred to the observation by Malcolm Turnball AC, Former Prime Minister of Australia that: 'Disrespecting women doesn't always result in violence against women but all violence against women begins with disrespecting women.'[71]

She said we need to think outside the box and mobilise supports at every level, and that leaders in the workplace play an important role in doing this. She told me that, years ago, Qantas flight attendants were trained on how to recognise the hallmarks of modern slavery and trafficking of women, who were being coerced onto flights. Leaders in the workplace have a similar role to these flight attendants. It's about being proactive.

As Georgie Dent passionately said at a 2020 event at my workplace:

Being weary is a luxury we can't afford. This is a state of emergency. Intimate partner violence is by far the deadliest form of terrorism on Australian soil. But there is hope. In the words of Margaet Mead: Never doubt that a small group of thoughtful, committed, citizens can change the world. Indeed, it is the only thing that ever has.

Key actions

Domestic and family violence is an issue that must be addressed by leaders and HR professionals to ensure humans in their workplaces are safe.

○ **IMPLEMENT A DFV POLICY.**

○ **OFFER INCREASED LEAVE OR BROADER BENEFITS** including parking, paid secure travel to and from work, short-term loans or accommodation support.

○ **TRAIN STAFF TO RESPOND SAFELY** and in a trauma-informed manner and offer supports.

○ **DEVELOP AND IMPLEMENT PERSONALISED SAFETY PLANS** for an emergency response to DFV.

○ **OFFER FLEXIBLE WORK ARRANGEMENTS**, such as adjustments to working hours or work locations.

○ **BE FLEXIBLE IN MANAGING THE PERFORMANCE** of employees experiencing DFV.

○ **DISCIPLINE PERPETRATORS OF VIOLENCE** who are using work time or resources and report to the police where evidence suggests this has occurred.

Chapter 6

Navigating uncertainty

It is well recognised and accepted that uncertainty can impact the mental health and wellbeing of humans. Restructures, change management and redundancies are a given in any workplace, especially during challenging economic times. We expect to see an increase in this type of activity in our workplaces during times of economic instability. However, an influx of complaints and disputes, and an increase in performance management and disciplinary action, often also proliferate during times of uncertainty.

This begs the question: is it the human whose performance is being scrutinised who has allowed their performance to slip? Or is their slip in performance a result of the challenging environment they are trying to perform in? As a leader or HR professional in this situation, you might wonder: has the change in workplace environment contributed to the issues you're seeing, or are humans who are feeling precarious in their employment raising complaints to avoid termination of their employment or increase their avenues for challenge if their job is on the line?

To address this, you must scan your environment, adopt forward-thinking strategies and nurture cultures that embrace change. Culture is the glue that holds compliance, policies, procedures, organisational systems, processes and decision-making together. Leaders who drive transformation need cultures of trust as their cornerstone. Change and innovation can only be built through autonomy, transparency, authenticity, collaboration, building trust and inspiring optimism in the future vision.

In times of uncertainty where employment ends, I see more legal challenges – humans seeking justice for perceived injustices; seeking compensation for loss or calling out their leaders' failings. People who can't quickly secure alternative employment and move forward when they leave a workplace tend to look back and seek revenge.

Interestingly I've also observed an increase in breaches of confidentiality and restraint provisions in these situations, as people who feel entitled to the fruits of their labour look to benefit and sabotage the organisation – or, more pointedly, the leader who has wronged them. This particularly occurs during times of economic uncertainty where people may find it difficult to obtain alternate employment and look for opportunities to take clients, information and ideas to competitors to increase their chances of new employment and success in the new role when they get there.

Burnout and substance abuse also rise during uncertain times, leading to an increase in misconduct by employees in and outside the workplace. Humans may go rogue with violence, aggression, bullying, harassment, theft and other forms of recalcitrance as they seek release from their stress and attempt to regain the control they feel they are losing.

Leaders who have seen an aggrieved former employee on a mission to bring them or their organisation down know the drain these individuals can be on the time, resources and energy of those involved. Leaders often become lost in these matters as they unfold and a person's quest for vindication becomes all-consuming. You can never predict when a bitter person with a grudge will cross your path and climb aboard the runaway train of complaints and litigation.

Whether people will feel aggrieved and vengeful often has little to do with what a leader actually says, but how the person feels when they walk out the door. To quote Maya Angelou, 'people will forget what you said, people will forget what you did, but people will never forget how you made them feel' – and this is especially the case when they're on their way out. Your actions will never matter more than how you treat people as they leave. That is their legacy. It makes or breaks people. It makes or breaks legal claims. It makes or breaks you as a leader or HR professional.

Compassion and respect in the execution of compliant legal processes will go a long way. There is no doubt the issues we deal with as employment lawyers are linked closely with both the economic environments the workplaces are running and the psychosocial impact of humans within them. Any consideration of how to address these issues and build healthy, respectful and inclusive workplaces that enable humans to thrive must consider these issues beyond baseline compliance. Therein lies the key to building safe, respectful, inclusive teams made up of thriving humans.

Key actions

Uncertainty increases risks to health and safety, disputes, complaints and legal claims.

○ **BE AWARE THAT DURING UNCERTAIN TIMES PEOPLE WILL FEEL MORE PRECARIOUS** and are more likely to make complaints and legal claims. Theft of confidential information and breaches of restraints are more likely to occur such that information security protocols should be put in place and closely monitored.

○ In uncertain times in particular, **COMMUNICATION WITH HUMANS AND A LINE OF SIGHT INTO THE FUTURE IS CRITICAL** to provide reassurance and build trust as far as possible.

○ During restructures, to the extent possible, **CUT JOBS ONCE** (and cut deep if necessary) to avoid people constantly looking over their shoulder fearful they will be next on the chopping block.

○ **BUILD TRUST AND BE A COMPASSIONATE LEADER**; this will help minimise risks and exposures.

Part II

SAFE AT WORK

Start with baseline compliance

Align with purpose, values and trust

Flourish with flexibility and inclusion

Enforce policies and exit jerks

Chapter 7

Start with baseline compliance

I made it clear from the outset that this book is not intended to be a crash course in how to ensure compliance with Australian workplace laws. These are admittedly complex, and legal advice is necessary to consider the needs of your workplace and the relevant legal frameworks that apply to them. This is the baseline necessary for the protection of the organisation and leaders within it from legal risk, liability and associated reputational damage.

Throughout this book I have however referenced some of the basics that are necessary to ensure compliance, including policies and procedures dealing with unlawful conduct, psychosocial hazards and burnout at work.

As a leader you must ensure policies and procedures are in place that are consistently and indiscriminately enforced. Complaint procedures are necessary to provide people with an avenue to report unlawful conduct, formally, informally or even anonymously. Responses to complaints must be trauma-informed, person-centred, timely and unbiased. This may mean external providers need to be engaged to undertake investigations into alleged conduct. Legal advice should be sought on disciplinary action that can and should follow if findings of unlawful conduct are substantiated. Not addressing unlawful conduct will increase legal liability for your organisation and you personally as a leader if you are involved in a contravention or allow unlawful conduct to occur on your watch.

Line managers need to be trained on what is required under the policies as they are often the first responders to these complaints. They are your human shield – they make or break whether an organisation will be compliant or exposed to significant liability. More importantly they are the custodians of human safety, and their treatment of people in your workplace and responses (or lack thereof) to issues as they arise can make or break the humans reporting to them.

Everyone in the workplace must also be trained on what is expected of them under the law. They must understand policies and procedures and know what they can do if they are subject to unlawful conduct. They must be reassured they are safe to speak up and will not be victimised for making complaints, and that they are encouraged to do so. They need to be reassured that, as their leader, you *will* act when they do. They should be encouraged to be active bystanders who do not tolerate unlawful conduct on their watch.

Compliance framework

While your compliance regime should be tailored to the nature and size of your workplace, industry and the specific risks associated with these, a starting point to guide you on a framework for proactive compliance and managing breaches is included in Figure 6.

FIGURE 6: FRAMEWORK FOR PROACTIVE COMPLIANCE AND MANAGING BREACHES

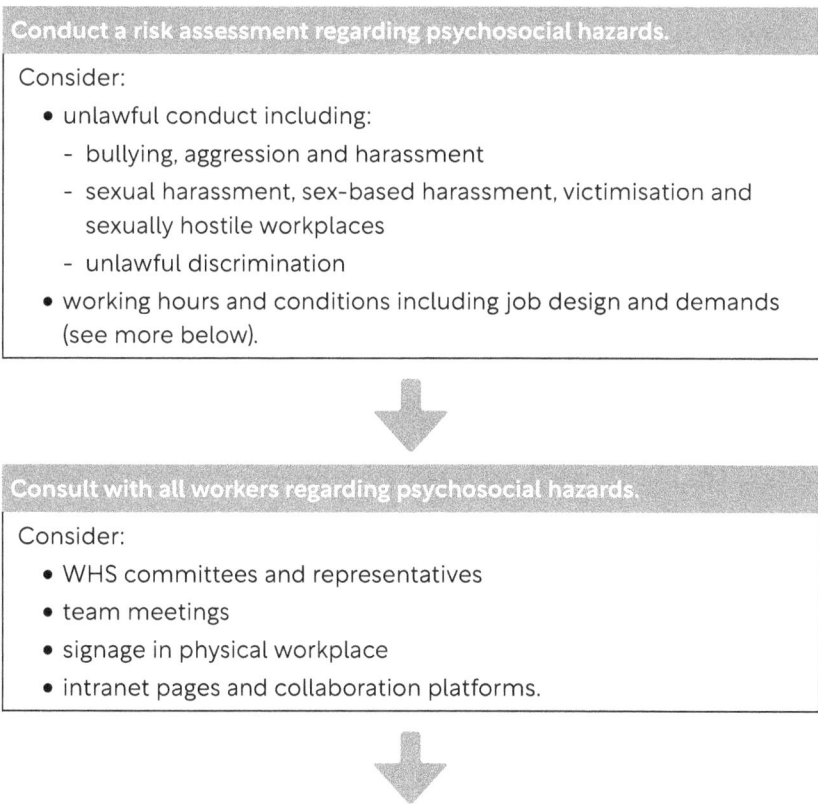

Conduct a risk assessment regarding psychosocial hazards.

Consider:
- unlawful conduct including:
  - bullying, aggression and harassment
  - sexual harassment, sex-based harassment, victimisation and sexually hostile workplaces
  - unlawful discrimination
- working hours and conditions including job design and demands (see more below).

Consult with all workers regarding psychosocial hazards.

Consider:
- WHS committees and representatives
- team meetings
- signage in physical workplace
- intranet pages and collaboration platforms.

Develop policies and procedures.

Policies that ensure compliance with legal obligations and issue lawful and reasonable directions to workers including in relation to:

- WHS including consultation and risk management procedures
- sexual harassment and unlawful conduct under SDA
- bullying, discrimination and other unlawful conduct
- complaint resolution procedure (including investigations and trauma-informed practices)
- flexible working policy and procedures
- DFV
- appropriate use of social media policy.

Leaders and HR professionals are cautioned to avoid overly prescriptive and onerous provisions in these policies and procedures that the organisation and its leaders may later come unstuck for not adhering to.

Provide practical, tailored and interactive training for all workers on policies and procedures.

Topics to cover include:

- what is, and what isn't, unlawful conduct
- expected behaviours
- consequences of breaches
- importance of bystander action
- how to make a complaint
- supports and resources available e.g. employee assistance program and other specialised counselling services
- reassurance of non-victimisation.

Consider:

- risks including safety, legal and reputational
- whether independent investigation should be undertaken by a third party or lawyer under legal professional privilege if:
  - there are insufficient skills and resources internally
  - there is a perception of bias
  - allegations relate to senior leaders in the organisation such that they cannot be impartially investigated
  - the allegations are serious and could result in significant consequences including investigation by regulators, prosecution under WHS laws or criminal charges
- suspension or alternate duties for alleged perpetrator and protection of complainant and all witnesses.

Ensure:

- a human-centred and trauma-informed approach to incidents, complaints and investigations (see the section later in the chapter on this)
- allegations are put to alleged perpetrator and there is procedural fairness during the investigation process
- employee assistance programs or other specialist support services are offered to all involved in investigation
- confidentiality and no victimisation.

If findings are substantiated, take disciplinary action.

Process should include:

- issuing a letter outlining the substantiated findings and breaches of policies or laws
- allowing an opportunity to respond in writing and in a follow-up meeting
- considering responses
- deciding whether termination of employment or other disciplinary action is warranted.

The process to be undertaken in this last section in particular depends on the seniority, remuneration, contract and remedies available to the alleged perpetrator. This process assumes the perpetrator is paid under the FWA high income threshold (set on 1 July each year) or otherwise covered by an award or enterprise agreement which gives them access to challenge the termination of their employment as an unfair dismissal. Legal advice should be obtained before proceeding with any termination of employment.

Assessing risks

The focus of this book has been on psychosocial hazards. In Part I we discussed at length the serious risks these pose for organisations and leaders and the serious consequences that can flow from them. In considering psychosocial hazards specific to your organisation, consider and assess risks arising from the following (without limitation):

- job demands
- low job control
- poor support
- lack of role clarity
- poor organisational change management
- inadequate reward and recognition
- poor organisational justice
- traumatic events or material
- remote or isolated work
- poor physical environment
- violence and aggression
- bullying

- harassment, including sexual and gender-based harassment, and
- conflict or poor workplace relationships and interactions.[72]

Safe Work Australia recommends the following steps for managing psychosocial hazards:

1. **IDENTIFY** psychological hazards and risks by:
   - talking and listening to workers (broadly defined to include contractors and volunteers)
   - inspecting your workplace
   - taking note of how people interact
   - reviewing reports and records
   - using a survey tool to gather information.

2. **ASSESS:** Consider what could happen if workers are exposed to the identified hazards and risks. Many hazards and their associated risks are well-known but some may need to be identified through a formal assessment process.

3. **CONTROL:** Where possible, eliminate the risk. This is always the safest option, but if it isn't possible, minimise the risk as much as possible through planning and prevention.

4. **REVIEW:** Maintain, monitor and review control measures when necessary. It is important to regularly review control measures to ensure they remain effective.[73]

Naturally, this process doesn't end once your workplace-specific risks are clearly identified and policies, procedures and processes are introduced to manage them. This is not a set-and-forget scenario but rather a continual process of monitoring, review and improvement to ensure humans remain safe at work.

Person-centred and trauma-informed practices

When it comes to complaint management, person-centred and trauma-informed practices (which I have always recommended as best-practice approaches) are now recommended for organisations to discharge their positive duty, including in the Australian Human Rights Commission's guidelines on complying with the Respect@Work laws.[74]

To adopt trauma-informed practices, leaders and HR professionals need to:

- understand trauma and its impacts
- support choice and control for the victim-survivor
- foster safe and trusting relationships where disclosures of trauma are possible and are responded to appropriately regardless of who the perpetrator is (including senior leaders, customers and third parties)
- adopt the following principles when responding to complaints:
  - prioritise safety, privacy and wellbeing of the victim-survivor and ensure their confidentiality is maintained
  - ensure all affected workers including witnesses and the alleged perpetrator have access to appropriate supports
  - listen to the victim-survivor in a compassionate, non-judgemental and sensitive manner

- give the victim-survivor input and choice, including the choice not to pursue a report (although as a leader or HR professional you must address as a far as a reasonably practicable risks arising from the matters you are on notice of)
- offer a range of options to the person who wants to report the unlawful behaviour (e.g. anonymously, over the phone, in-person) and give them choice about how to resolve a report to the extent possible whilst also ensuring they and others are safe at work
- handle reports fairly, impartially and reasonably in accordance with procedural fairness principles ensuring that all participants in the process have clear information about the process and how procedural fairness will be upheld
- ensure responses are provided in a timely manner and keep all parties informed of the process (communication and transparency is key to building trust in the system even where it's not perfect)
- understand recovery is possible for everyone.[75]

In essence, trauma-informed practices provide the agency, choice, compassion, support and hope necessary for victim-survivors to trust the system and survive it.

Lessons from the law

For years leaders have felt caught between a rock and a hard place: trying to ensure the health and safety of humans in their workplace by addressing bullying, sexual harassment, discrimination and other unlawful and toxic behaviours, while also trying to avoid being dragged through courts and tribunals for unfair dismissal cases and other legal claims when they exit a perpetrator for unlawful conduct.

There are countless matters that provide illustrative examples of the conduct we discuss in this book and the responses of Australian courts and tribunals to them. Sometimes employers win, sometimes they lose. As employment lawyers we always learn from these cases, which is why I would like to share some examples with you here.

These examples demonstrate how courts and tribunals have responded to cases involving inappropriate and unlawful conduct at work. My aim here is not to provide an outline, as a legal text-book would – of the war and peace of legal jurisprudence and case precedents – but rather to demonstrate the many manifestations of the human condition, the unfortunate events that result in court cases and the evolving views of our judiciary on dysfunctional behaviours in the workplace. Note all but the last of these cases emerged before the Respect@Work laws were passed, and before the more recent changes to the *FWA* incorporating the prohibition on sexual harassment. They demonstrate how judicial thinking emerged to meet prevailing community standards even before the legislation caught up. They also provide reassurance that our courts and tribunals are no longer tolerating jerks at work – and neither should you.

Sexual harassment claims

The following cases are notable decisions relating to successful claims made under the *SDA* by victim-survivors of sexual harassment and demonstrate the courts' approach to liability, vicarious liability for employers and damages for these claims.

Court said community standards changed (a decade ago)[76]

In a landmark case before three judges in the Full Court of the Federal Court of Australia (FCAFC) a decade ago, a judgement of a $18,000 in damages as compensation for breach of the *SDA* was overturned and replaced with an order for the respondent to pay the sum of $130,000 and the costs of the appeal.

Richardson was working for Oracle as a consulting manager and Tucker was working as a sales representative. Richardson's case was based on the allegation that, from the time of her first meeting with Tucker, she was subjected to a humiliating series of slurs, alternating with sexual advances, which built into a constant barrage of sexual harassment. She gave evidence of 11 incidents, each said to amount to sexual harassment and together evidencing a pattern of unlawful conduct.

The inappropriate comments made to Richardson by Tucker included:

- 'Rebecca, you and I fight so much ... I think we must have been married in our last life.'
- 'So, Rebecca, how do you think our marriage was? I bet the sex was hot.'
- 'You know you love me.'

Richardson made a number of complaints about Oracle's investigation of Tucker's conduct and its aftermath including that:

- her complaint centred on an alleged need for a 'formal complaint'
- Oracle required her to continue to work with Tucker while the investigation was carried out
- she was restricted from discussing the matter with colleagues while the investigation was being carried out.

The trial judge substantially accepted Richardson's evidence and rejected Tucker's denials and attempts to defend his conduct as 'unintended, misunderstood or innocuous' and found that Oracle was vicariously liable for Tucker's conduct.

The trial judge assessed the damages to be awarded to Richardson as compensation for Tucker's sexual harassment at only $18,000 and did not accept any economic loss was 'caused' by the sexual harassment because Richardson resigned and secured another job within a month, albeit at less pay.

The landmark decision on appeal

The FCAFC referenced the finding of the trial judge that the 'initial exchange marked the beginning of a pattern of behaviour which was to continue over a period of months' and held:

A repeated pattern in [these] encounters was behaviour by Mr Tucker consistent with the thesis that he was trying to get the upper hand in his relationship with Ms Richardson. Some of those attempts were at least smutty, some were offensive and some (expressed more privately) involved initiatives representing a more direct interest of a sexual kind. When they occurred in the hearing of others they seemed consistently humiliating.

In overturning the damages sum of $18,000 the FCAFC, featuring recently retired Justice Kenny in one of the most widely reported and impactful decisions of her career, held:

I consider that, having regard to the nature and extent of Ms Richardson's injuries and prevailing community stand- ards, the low level of the damages awarded by the trial judge itself bespeaks error ...

In searching for the standard against which to measure the 'manifest inadequacy' of an award of damages for sexual harassment, the same, or similar, matters must be taken into account. Pain and suffering, hurt and humiliation and, more generally, the deprivation of the enjoyment of life have no market value: pain and suffering and money are in this sense incommensurable.

After analysing damages awards in discrimination cases at length as compared to other personal injury cases, the court increased the general damages award from $18,000 to $100,000 and ordered a further $30,000 in economic loss based on the difference between Richardson's salary at Oracle and the new employer for a period of two years, finding there was a connection between the sexual harassment and this loss, despite her resignation. The court held:

> Even this cursory overview of the quantum of awards historically awarded in these other fields to successful claimants in situations not wholly unlike Ms Richardson's reveals a substantial disparity between the level of those awards and the typical compensatory damages provided to victims of sexual discrimination and harassment. Such disparity bespeaks the fact that today an award for sexual harassment, though within the accepted range for such cases, may be manifestly inadequate as compensation for the damage suffered by the victim, judged by reference to prevailing community standards.

A very grave example of sexual harassment'[77]

The principal of a firm was found to have engaged in sexual harassment against a former employee, Hill, in breach of the *SDA*.

The principal subjected Hill to sexual harassment that included:

- entering her bedroom on the evening of a Sydney work trip in his underwear and then re-entering her room the following morning and watching her get dressed
- coercing hugs from her on a number of occasions by

blocking her exit and putting her in a position where she felt she could not decline

- sending many emails raising personal details about her and signing off with 'love' or hugs and kisses despite her assertions that she did not want to be in an intimate relationship with him
- sending emails with veiled threats that her employment depended upon her entering a sexual or romantic relationship with him.

The findings

Hill was awarded $120,000 in general damages and $50,000 in aggravated damages.

In a contemptuous judgement of what was described as a 'very grave example of sexual harassment' the court held:

> [The principal] was a solicitor who not only should know the law but should conduct himself in a very high standard befitting of his position in society. [The principal] is supposed to uphold the law. The law prohibits the very behaviour in which [the principal], a lawyer, indulged … it is my view that the conduct of [the principal] is a very grave example of sexual harassment.

During his evidence, the principal suggested he was not making sexual advances but, rather, attempting to pursue a romantic relationship. He pointed to several passages in his emails, an example of which was, to the effect, 'I want to be your lover and I am keeping my heart open for you.' In response to this it was held:

> [The principal] is attempting to differentiate an advance that is nothing more than sexual in nature against his proposal of a deeper, loving relationship. The distinction advanced reflects a social myopia on the part of [the principal] that, thankfully, is not reflected in the Act.

In making orders for aggravated general damages, his honour made the following observations about what was described by Hill's counsel as 'slut shaming'. His honour said he would not use that term but could describe the principal's claim as 'utterly outrageous', noting:

> [The principal] attempted to put the blame for his behaviour upon [Hill] describing her as flirty and coquet-tish. In his statement, he has described a number of occasions that [Hill] wore alluring dresses to the office. In other parts, he describes the perfume that she wore. In other parts he describes that he could see her bra and part of her breasts when looking at the neckline in her dress. [The principal] described [Hill] as 'encouraging' his behaviour because of those things. **It is the mark of a bygone era where women, by their mere presence, were responsible for the reprehensible behaviour of men. The Sex Discrimination Act was enacted to help eliminate this sort of thinking.**

The principal had the audacity to appeal this decision but his pleas for leniency were not met with sympathy from the Full Bench, which held:

> It is conduct of the most reprehensible kind ... she made it repeatedly plain that she was not interested in a romantic relationship ... There was nothing ambiguous about her behaviour. [He] made a welcome of rejection ... At trial, he sought to contend that she had behaved around him in a 'coquettish' fashion ... In my opinion, the trial judge was correct to condemn [his] conduct of the trial as, in effect, a continuation of his harassment ... This appeal is devoid of merit and I would infer was pursued for the same purpose. Some of the submissions were, in my opinion, insulting. It should not have been brought and, in my opinion, should be emphatically dismissed.

Unfair dismissal claims

The following cases provide illustrative examples of decisions where perpetrators of unlawful conduct in the workplace have challenged the termination of their employment in the Fair Work Commission's unfair dismissal jurisdiction, on the basis the termination of their employment was harsh, unjust or unreasonable. They lost.

Team leader rightly sacked for 'blatant benevolent sexism'[78]

The termination of a paint shop group leader was upheld on the basis he engaged in 'blatant benevolent sexism' and unacceptable behaviour towards a group of young, female fixed-term contractors, which created a 'weird and dirty atmosphere'.

Toyota dismissed the paint shop group leader after 23 years of employment, after investigating an anonymous complaint accusing him of inappropriate behaviour and sexual harassment. In the termination letter, Toyota said the group leader fostered an 'exclusionary culture' and engaged in conduct that breached its policies including the shared values expressed as the 'Toyota Way'.

The leader argued he was merely 'a nice friendly guy' and that his dismissal was disproportionate to the gravity of his misconduct, and harsh given his 23-year unblemished history at Toyota.

The findings

It was accepted the group leader would encourage young female employees to sit on his lap, or on the arm of his chair, while he was seated in it. His claim that his chair was 'king size' and could comfortably accommodate young female employees either side of him was held to be unfeasible after a site visit with the Commissioner to, among other things, test out the chair.

The Commissioner found:

It is simply inconceivable in a workplace in the current era that behaviour of this nature by a group leader, who has the responsibility of leading a group of young employees regardless of gender, would be condoned.

By allowing behaviours of such a nature to take place it is evident the working environment, although not hostile, was uncomfortable for some and at the very least was an unhealthy work environment ... The comments made by [the group leader] to the young female [temporary fixed-term] employees in my view were in fact a rather blatant form of benevolent sexism which has no place in the workplace.

The group leader's evidence was 'self-serving and designed to deflect from his own unacceptable behaviour'.

The group leader submitted that the dismissal had very serious financial consequences as if his employment had not been terminated for misconduct, he would have been entitled to receive a substantial redundancy package. He argued that as a 50-year-old man he was not likely to find comparable work in the future due to the demise of the car industry. The Commissioner was:

not persuaded that the mitigating circumstances outweigh the seriousness of the conduct ... He was responsible for a group of vulnerable young female employees whose future employment was reliant on his approval ... He was responsible for developing and encouraging an environment in which inappropriate behaviour was expected and encouraged and even at the hearing demonstrated a complete lack of remorse or recognition of the seriousness of his conduct. I do not consider that his dismissal was harsh in those circumstances.

The lessons

People accused of harassment, particularly those in more senior roles, cannot rely on an absence of complaints about their behaviour to suggest it wasn't unwelcome or inappropriate.

The group leader's defence was not plausible where his behaviour was directed towards workers who were temporary fixed-term employees and where their future employability relied on his approval.

How can it be said they did not object in all those circumstances? There was disproportionality between the role and authority that he had, and their own future.

The case serves as a reminder and warning on the dangers of 'subcultures' developing in organisations, where employers operate across different sites and with different styles of leadership. The workers in this case were isolated and the leaders left to their own devices. A subculture had developed that was completely contrary to the values that Toyota had at the senior leadership and HR level.

Toyota's investigation of the behaviour was prompted by an anonymous call to its 'STOPline' about a different relationship (that was in another unfair dismissal matter accepted as being consensual), which then morphed into this case. When these subcultures do develop, it only takes one complaint about one incident for the whole situation to unravel. This case also demonstrates the importance of providing a confidential and independent reporting mechanism for workers who may be vulnerable, isolated and who otherwise may feel unsafe and uncomfortable raising a complaint.

Racism not 'good-hearted banter'[79]

What a misguided worker claimed to be just 'good-hearted banter' brought his 17-year tenure to an end with the Fair Work Commission supporting the employer's decision for an on-the-spot dismissal.

The Fair Work Commission upheld the summary dismissal of a StarTrack forklift driver for directing vicious and violent racial slurs at colleagues.

The employee argued that:

- no-one had complained about the comments
- the comments were 'good-hearted banter' between colleagues
- the comments were enjoyed by others

- it was just comedy and humour
- the phrases were terms of endearment.

The findings

In finding a valid reason for the termination the Fair Work Commission said:

> *Such an attempted defence or justification of abhorrent behaviour is an approach that disregards the fundamental wrongdoing, and it fails to appreciate that the victims of the wrongdoing do not complain because they feel powerless to prevent the conduct.*

The Fair Work Commission found that taking the approach that language was not offensive because no-one had complained 'has regrettable and disturbing parallels with the recent exposure of incidents of sexual harassment in the employment context, which has created what is referred to as the #MeToo movement'.

The Fair Work Commission also observed the employee:

> *seemed to be unable to appreciate that the racial components of his workplace 'banter' and swearing was separate and distinguishable from any robust language or verbal jousting that may be used as 'part and parcel' of a 'knockabout' workplace.*

In simple terms, a line is crossed when race or ethnicity is included in any communications with co-workers, and any suggestion of being well intentioned does not provide a defence or justification for conduct that is fundamentally unacceptable.

On this basis, the Fair Work Commission distinguished that 'crudity can be tolerated, racism cannot'.

While the worker's situation, including his long service, age and otherwise unblemished record, might have established some basis for giving him a second chance, he 'failed to appreciate the fundamental misfeasance associated with the use of racial slurs in any context or circumstances' and showed 'little or no remorse'.

In all the circumstances, and particularly given the employer's zero-tolerance policy for racism – which included a training video titled 'Expect Respect' – in its culturally and ethnically diverse workforce, the Fair Work Commission was 'not prepared to disturb the balanced and properly considered determination made by the employer'.

The lessons

Leaders should act promptly to address race discrimination at work and should consider, subject to legal advice on specific circumstances, take a hard line and terminate the employment of perpetrators of racism immediately (without notice of termination or pay in lieu) for serious and wilful misconduct. The employer's position is particularly strengthened where they have in place policies relating to appropriate workplace conduct, they have provided training in relation to those policies, an appropriate investigation has been conducted that substantiates that policies and/or laws have been breached, and a disciplinary process has been followed prior to termination of employment.

'Sexual harassment has no place in the workplace'[80]

In a recent decision, an advanced mechanical tradesperson was summarily dismissed from a refinery in Western Australia after almost 20 years of service after an investigation into allegations of sexual harassment. The male employee was accused of touching a female coworker, as they passed each other in an office in 'an intimate location' in a way which made her jump and make a noise although she tried to avoid 'making a scene'.

The female employee was reluctant to report the incident due to fear of 'backlash' from other employees but cooperated in the investigation after it was brought to the employer's attention by another employee.

After being summarily dismissed, the male employee commenced unfair dismissal proceedings, alleging the conduct was accidental, due to the female employee standing in a narrow walkway, and not done with sexual intent. At the hearing, it was revealed the applicant was previously investigated and counselled about similar allegations.

The female employee had to be ordered to provide evidence in the Fair Work Commission and her name was de-identified in the decision.

The findings

Deputy President Binet rejected the male employee's case noting he and his representatives sadly 'took a well-worn but discredited path of blaming the victim for the contact'. She further noted the fact the female employee did not make a formal complaint and was reluctant to voluntarily give evidence at the hearing removed 'any suggestion that she fabricated or over-dramatised the event maliciously to place [the male employee] at risk of disciplinary action'.

It was held, whether there was sexual intent or not, the action was of sexual nature, which was serious misconduct warranting dismissal stating:

> 'Amendments to the FW Act which specially identity sexual harassment as a valid reason for dismissal reflect a societal recognition that sexual harassment has no place in the workplace in the same way as violence or theft.'

The male employee's conduct was found to have been clearly in breach of the employer's Code and policies governing behaviour in the workplace. He should have been aware of those policies as he had a contractual obligation to read and comply with them and he was provided with opportunities to be trained on them. In a damning decision reflecting the decreased appetite of bench members of the Fair Work Commission to tolerate jerks, the Deputy President said:

'In any event, [the] policies merely reflect modern day societal expectations about behaviour. The bar as to what constitutes consent for physical and sexual interactions has been significantly raised in the broader community. An even higher bar has been set for interactions occurring in work related environments. The media coverage and social discourse in relation these issues has been extensive, placing those in Australian workplaces on notice that their behaviour will attract greater scrutiny and face higher standards than in the past. This is particularly so in the mining industry in Western Australia where a parliamentary inquiry focused community attention on the odious frequency of sexual harassment and assault of women in the mining industry.'

The unfair dismissal case was dismissed.

The lessons

The case is yet another example of the importance of appropriate policies and procedures, contractual provisions and training to reinforce standards of expected conduct and support decisions to terminate the employment of employees in breach of those provisions. This case also shows the reduced tolerance by the Fair Work Commission (and other courts as demonstrated earlier in this chapter) for victim blaming by perpetrators and their representatives. At the time of writing this book, it is the most recent case demonstrating the intolerance of the Fair Work Commission for sexual harassment and jerks in the workplace regardless of an employee's length of service or intentions.

Key actions

Organisations and leaders need to ensure their compliance framework is adequately set up to minimise risks and exposures arising from breach of state and federal discrimination laws and WHS laws, while also successfully defending unfair dismissal claims when they do exit perpetrators. The law and courts are no longer tolerating the intolerable. This provides reassurance for leaders disciplining those who engage in unlawful conduct.

○ **CONSULT WITH WORKERS AND UNDERTAKE RISK ASSESSMENTS** focused on the specific psychosocial hazards in your workplace.

○ **DEVELOP CONTROL MEASURES** to eliminate or minimise psychosocial hazards as far as reasonably practicable.

○ **ENSURE YOU HAVE MULTIPLE AVENUES AVAILABLE FOR PEOPLE TO MAKE COMPLAINTS** including anonymous and informal complaints and give humans agency in how these are managed by adopting trauma-informed practices.

○ **PROMPTLY AND INDEPENDENTLY INVESTIGATE BREACHES OF POLICIES AND PROCEDURES** and consider, in matters involving senior leaders or serious consequences, whether a lawyer should be engaged to commission the investigation process under legal professional privilege.

○ **CONSIDER LESSONS FROM CASE LAW** and promptly act on inappropriate conduct balancing the requirements to ensure procedural fairness for the alleged perpetrator and the need to ensure the health and safety of all humans in your workplace as your main priority where these obligations conflict.

○ **CONSIDER THE PROCESS FROM THE OUTSET** with reference to the seniority, remuneration, industrial instrument coverage, contract and remedies available to the alleged perpetrator. Specifically, consider whether a termination with notice (for loss of trust and confidence rather than serious and wilful misconduct) should be considered for perpetrators not covered by the unfair dismissal jurisdiction to avoid the time, cost and disruption of an investigation if this is preferred and appropriate after seeking legal advice.

○ **TAKE SOME COMFORT FROM THE DECISIONS OF THE FAIR WORK COMMISSION** in making decisions to exit perpetrators (see more in Chapter 10).

○ In a contest between procedural deficiencies that may risk an unfair dismissal claim (where reinstatement is very rarely awarded and the maximum compensation is six months' pay up to a jurisdictional cap that increase every year) and the health and safety of workers (where criminal penalties apply), **ALWAYS PUT SAFETY FIRST.**

Chapter 8

Align with purpose, values and trust

There are countless definitions of workplace culture and discussions of what it is, should be and could be. The simplest and most appropriate definition for the purpose of this book is that culture is the shared values, belief system, attitudes and the set of assumptions that people in a workplace share.[81]

As Simon Sinek said, 'Great companies don't hire skilled people and motivate them, they hire already motivated people and inspire them.' A positive workplace culture is created when humans galvanise to achieve an organisation's mission while living their shared values. When this works, not only do humans thrive but so do organisations.

A national survey of 1544 employees conducted by R U OK? in partnership with the Centre for Corporate Health revealed that workplace conflict, coupled with employee and manager relationship problems, could adversely affect employee mental health and wellbeing to the extent that many felt unequipped to address the issues and instead looked for support elsewhere.[82] The survey found that 46 per cent of people would rather look for a new job than contend with a workplace issue, while 48 per cent resorted to taking days off when faced with a tough time at work.

The upshot: if you have a poor culture, you lose your best humans and disengage the rest of them.

Figure 7 represents the benefits of a positive culture, highlighting how it helps to achieve key performance indicators. The fundamental ingredient that underpins these cultures is trust. Ultimately, more trust means less stress at work, and reduced workplace turnover.

FIGURE 7: THE BENEFITS OF A POSITIVE CULTURE

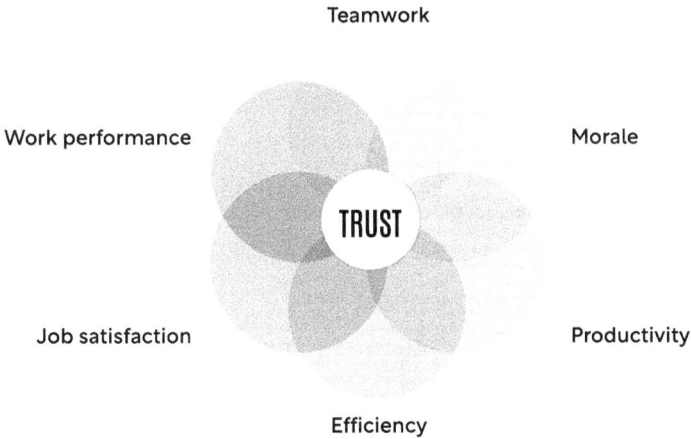

Teamwork

Work performance

Morale

TRUST

Job satisfaction

Productivity

Efficiency

Trust at work

In Chapter 2 we discussed how destructive fear and blame can be to humans and psychological safety at work. The antithesis of fear is trust. Trust is vital; it's the magic ingredient to ensure humans thrive and organisations prosper. It acts as both the lubrication that keeps organisations running smoothly as well as the glue that holds it all together. Research has shown high levels of trust in organisations leads to higher revenue, profit, innovation and engagement, and lower costs related to turnover, accidents, sick leave and theft.[83] In contrast, low levels of trust marked by managerial surveillance causes employees to be more prone to engage in deviant behaviour (such as time theft, inattentiveness, cyberslacking, tardiness and so on) and a decrease in performance.[84]

Neuroeconomist Dr Paul Zak says trust is the magic ingredient and key to ensuring humans are safe at work. His research found that, compared with humans at low-trust organisations, those at high-trust organisations reported:

- 74 per cent less stress
- 106 per cent more energy at work
- 50 per cent higher productivity
- 13 per cent fewer sick days
- 76 per cent more engagement
- 29 per cent more satisfaction with their lives
- 40 per cent less burnout.[85]

Given these findings it is clear trust benefits everyone in the workplace and is the key to building a safe and productive organisation where humans thrive.

Dr Paul Zak and his colleague Dr Kenneth Nowack say the following two elements have biological effects on humans driven by oxytocin, creating environments where humans trust each other:

1. **interpersonal trust:** the extent to which I will give you the benefit of the doubt about your behaviour

2. **psychological safety:** the extent to which I believe you will give me the benefit of the doubt about my behaviour[86]

Based on their research, Figure 8 outlines the key behaviours you need to demonstrate as a leader to build interpersonal trust and psychological safety with humans in your workplace.

FIGURE 8: KEY LEADERSHIP BEHAVIOURS TO BUILD TRUST

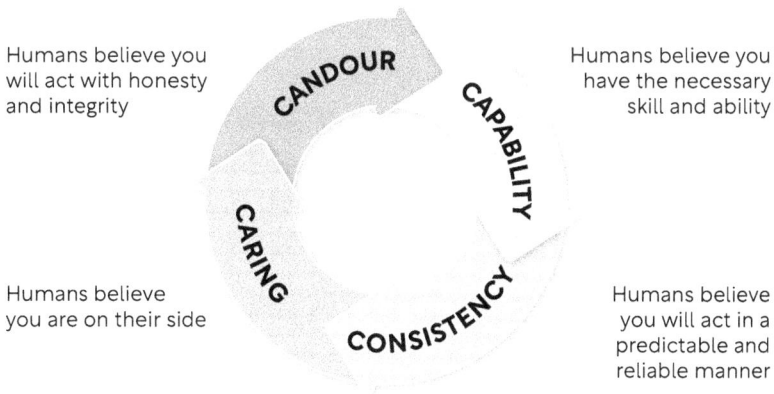

Humans believe you will act with honesty and integrity

CANDOUR

Humans believe you have the necessary skill and ability

CAPABILITY

CARING

Humans believe you are on their side

CONSISTENCY

Humans believe you will act in a predictable and reliable manner

Adapted from Nowack and Zak 2020[87]

Social skills are critical to creating stronger bonds of relational connection that results in higher levels of trust with humans. Connection not only addresses the problem of loneliness and its ill effects, but it also builds trust. When humans see that as their leader you are acting with goodwill and you have their best interests at heart, they are more likely to trust you.

Trust is built when humans feel valued at work, are given autonomy, believe that leaders care about their wellbeing and feel safe to make mistakes without being blamed. Reframing mistakes as learning opportunities and adopting the growth mindset we have discussed was also found by Dr Nowack as being critical to trust. It's about creating cultures focused on experimentation rather than failure and encouraging shared accountability.[88]

Leading with trust, not control

The world has changed. The nature of work has changed. Where we work has changed. We are moving between jobs faster than ever before and between tasks at a pace more rapid than we ever contemplated. We are constantly 'on' – on email, on smart devices, on social media and on the job. The parameters of the workplace are also infinitely evolving as boundaries erode, while advancements in 'big brother' style technology enable minute-by-minute remote surveillance. This is met with considerable resistance and costs to trust and in turn, workplace culture and morale. All the while, from a legal perspective, risk is increasing for organisations and leaders who are finding themselves increasingly scrutinised and exposed for action they take (or don't take) in the course of their duties.

As a leader in this new world of work, you are caught in a conundrum – how do you 'control' increased risk and liability while simultaneously encouraging initiative, flexibility, autonomy and creativity to drive workforce engagement and to attract and retain future generations of talent? An entrepreneurial, purpose and values-driven culture is critical to engagement of the workforce of the future, and any attempt to reign in or enforce rigid controls over future generations will not only be resisted but will disengage and alienate a significant pool of talent.

Leaders and HR professionals, as guided by lawyers, have for decades been risk and compliance-driven, focused on finding things that can go wrong or result in legal exposure and then enforcing rules, policies and procedures to seal exposure gaps. Non-compliance with rules, codes of conduct, policies or procedures leads to disciplinary action including termination of employment such that humans are forced to comply due to fear of reprimand.

In the changing and increasingly autonomous and creative world of work, successful leaders rely less on control-based prescriptive policies and fear-driven compliance initiatives and more on providing humans with environments where leaders inspire engagement and achieve buy-in to a core purpose and values.

The risks associated with litigation in our industrial system, the paramount obligation to ensure the health and safety of workers and the vicarious liability organisations bear for unlawful conduct are such that we simply cannot do away with policies and proce-dures altogether without significantly increasing risk and legal exposure. However, leaders and HR professionals must rethink overly prescriptive control-based polices and redefine compliance obligations by connecting them to core purpose and values-based ideologies. This is what will influence and inspire humans to commit to them.

The key to high-performing teams is to unite the workforce with trust, psychological safety and common purpose, and consistently reinforce core values and ideologies that are intrinsically instilled. This will mean humans are inspired to do the right thing even when no-one is watching. It is only with this foundation that leaders can confidently encourage autonomy and flexibility so creativity and innovation can flourish.

Media reports are proving every day that trust in government, leadership and industry has eroded to an all-time low. Hard to earn and easy to lose, trust is the core of positive, healthy, high-performance workplace cultures and good leadership. Trust is the superpower of successful workplaces.

Given humans are our best ambassadors, leaders can benefit as much from curiosity about humans and how to engage them as they can from knowledge of compliance requirements. To be an effective leader, you need to develop an intuition about humans that enables you to not only see issues and risks, but to understand why they have materialised. Instead of commanding and controlling, focus on building trust, psychological safety and creating respectful and inclusive workplace cultures, playing to human strengths, encouraging authenticity and creativity.

Thriving with purpose

The pandemic has driven burnout, inspired lateral career moves and caused staff retention rates to plummet. Humans are re-evaluating their work against more holistic criteria such as engagement, culture fit and job satisfaction. Leaders and HR professionals should focus less on *where* humans work but rather provide direction and inspiration on *why* people work.

Purpose is a tricky thing to dictate. As a leader you need to consider and embed the 'why' into recruiting, onboarding and performance management. Humans have a range of passions and motivations. As a leader you can cultivate an energised workforce by supporting people to draw a link between their intrinsic motivators and the functions of the business.

Good leaders don't tell people what to do in granular detail, they explain why they're doing what they're doing. They explain where the person's role fits within the bigger picture – why it's important, and how it will help achieve the team's overall objectives and in turn the organisation's purpose and then empower them with supported autonomy.

We learnt in Part I of this book that fear leads to stress, exhaustion, burnout and resentment. Fear leads to broken humans in the workplace. As a leader you need to create an environment where humans feel safe to unpack mistakes by encouraging a growth mindset and framing mistakes as learning opportunities. Productive conversations do not happen when humans are in fight-or-flight mode. Vulnerability from leaders is critical to create safe spaces. That means holding the mirror up when you've made mistakes and leading by example on how you foster a growth mindset. Leaders need to reassure humans working for them that they won't let perfect be the enemy of good.

When humans fall short of expectations, feedback is best delivered within the framework of the organisation's purpose and values. What flow-on effect does this work have on the team or clients? Be constructive and focus on the task, not the individual. Play the ball, not the human. Humans need to understand the parameters within their control to empower them to start achieving results.

The humans working for you are your greatest resource and asset. Ensuring their wellbeing and creating environments where they thrive is the key to your success as a leader and the success of your organisation. Lead with purpose to achieve this by being strategic with outputs. Humans cannot be firing on all cylinders all the time. Inevitably, there will be deadlines that call for a big sprint. But once that job is done, your people need to conserve and replenish energy so when the next hard deadline presents, they are ready to hit the ground running.

High-performance athletes work in cycles of intense training and recovery and build-up to their next intense period focused at all times on the next goal they are seeking to achieve as a step towards their overall goal and purpose. In the same way, high-performing teams in the workplace need to prioritise endurance and focus on purpose. Collaboration and careful workforce planning are required to ensure more even workflows so that some people don't burn out while others are underutilised and demoralised. We are working harder than ever before, and our working life has significantly extended. Now, more than ever, work is a marathon not a sprint.

Key actions

As humans are working harder for longer, it is important we create safe and supportive environments that inspire and energise them to survive the marathon.

○ **BUILD TRUST AND PSYCHOLOGICAL SAFETY** as the vital ingredients required to ensure humans are safe at work.

○ **FOCUS ON PURPOSE** and *why* humans work. Do not micromanage. Inspire humans with broad objectives they are to achieve as a team and provide them with supported autonomy to achieve.

○ **FOSTER AND ENCOURAGE A GROWTH MINDSET** by framing mistakes as learning opportunities and create safe spaces by showing vulnerability as a leader.

Chapter 9

Flourish with flexibility and inclusion

For well over 15 years, I have advocated for flexibility as being imperative to the creation of diverse and inclusive workplaces. Inclusive workplaces undeniably enhance organisational effectiveness, competitive advantage, decision-making, morale and performance, and deliver higher returns to shareholders.

Flex at work

As the world of work has changed, humans are increasingly working remotely and the four walls of the workplace are evaporating. Flexible working arrangements are increasingly becoming adjustments that can be reasonably accommodated – not only without hardship to organisations, but indeed with improved productivity and efficiencies.

After years of assisting employers grappling with the implementation of flexible work and advocating for the benefits of healthy and inclusive workplaces, the move to flexible work as the new normal has certainly been an evolution. Research undertaken by the Committee for Economic Development of Australia (CEDA) released in 2024 confirmed, as expected, that more parents, people with a disability, people with health conditions, and carers have joined the workforce as a result of the post-pandemic shift to flexible working, as well as a strong labour market.[89]

Further, analysis of Household Income and Labor Dynamics in Australia Survey data found that from 2019 to 2022, workforce participation in jobs where people could work from home increased by:

- 8.5 per cent for women with young children
- nearly 6 per cent for people with a disability or health conditions.[90]

This represents monumental progress in workplace participation and inclusion of these diverse groups. It does, however, beg the question: what happens to these humans now that some CEOs and leaders are insisting on a return to the office, and there is a concerted push by some parts of the business community to return to the way things were pre-pandemic? These humans are entitled to legal protections, as I will outline below; but for years we have advocated for structural changes to mainstream flexibility – because when everyone is working flexibly, diverse, vulnerable and underrepresented groups in the workplace are less likely to be adversely affected for doing so.

The legal baseline

The National Employment Standard in the *FWA* applies to all employees covered by the national workplace relations system and includes a right for employees who meet the following eligibility requirements:

- permanent employees who have completed at least 12 months of continuous service with their employer immediately before making the request; or
- casual employees who have been employed by the employer on a regular and systematic basis for a sequence of periods of employment of at least 12 months immediately before making the request and who have a reasonable expectation of continuing employment by the employer on a regular and systematic basis.

Eligible employees are entitled to request a change in their working arrangements if they also have any of the following protected attributes:

- are the parent, or have responsibility for the care, of a child who is of school age or younger
- are a carer within the meaning of the *Carer Recognition Act 2010*
- have a disability
- are 55 or older
- are experiencing violence from a member of their family

- provide care or support to a member of their immediate family or household, who requires care or support because they are experiencing violence from their family.

Changes in working arrangements may be to the:

- hours of work including reduced hours and changes in start and finish times;
- patterns of work such as job sharing or split shifts; and/or
- location of work including working from home.

Employers can only refuse such a request on 'reasonable business grounds'. Employers must give employees a written response to their request within 21 days, stating whether they grant or refuse the request. If the employer refuses the request, the written response must include the reasons for the refusal which employees can, following the introduction of more recent changes to the law, challenge in the Fair Work Commission.

It is unlawful under the *FWA* to take adverse action against an employee including termination (with civil penalties for breaches) for making a flexible work request or discriminate against employees based on the protected attributes outlined above.

Whether a refusal to accommodate such requests is unreasonable will depend on the facts and circumstances of the situation. A defence is available to employers on the basis that an adjustment is not reasonable if it would cause an unjustifiable hardship on the employer taking all circumstances into account, including consideration of:

- the benefits of the arrangement to the employee, other staff and clients
- the effects on the employer and all the people involved if they don't provide the arrangement
- the costs involved relative to their financial circumstances.

Reasonable grounds for refusal for a small employer may differ vastly to those that are reasonable for a large, well-resourced employer. In a post-Covid world, what may have once been 'unreasonable' may not be anymore.

Further, the consequences for failing to accommodate flexible work arrangements have also increased, with changes the *FWA* in 2023 providing the Fair Work Commission with the power to scrutinise whether the business grounds upon which an employer refuses a flexible work arrangement are in fact 'reasonable'. This has resulted in applications flowing into the Commission from employees relating to refusal to accommodate flexible work arrangements. These matters are conciliated in the first instance but if conciliation is unsuccessful they proceed to arbitration, where the Commission makes a binding decision about the working arrangements. Invariably this is resulting in more employers accommodating requests in the first instance, when an application is threatened or at conciliation, as there is a reluctance to have the Commission consider and scrutinise a decision about one employee's work arrangements that may have a lasting impact on the employer's arrangements with its entire workforce.

Fear versus benefit factors of flexibility

Despite decades of data on the benefits of flexible working and evidence of these arrangements upholding business continuity for organisations and financial security for workers during the pandamic, the reluctance to unreservedly embrace flexible working as the way of the future persists across many organisations.

Embracing flexibility requires an adjustment to not only the way an organisation operates, but also how it thinks. Properly implementing flexible work practices involves challenging assumptions about how things must be done and coming up with new and innovative ways of utilising staff. Rigidity, inflexibility, fear of loss of 'control' and not knowing what to do or how to do it were major psychological barriers for organisations and leaders reticent to embrace or continue remote working in particular.

As the dust has settled post-pandemic, we have seen many leaders start to creep back to old habits and media reports of CEOs and leaders insisting on a return to the office or physical workplace. The Fair Work Commission's power to arbitrate flexible work requests provides some fear factor for employers and leaders to accom-modate requests, but this is limited only to employees who have protected attributes and meet the eligibility requirements to request such arrangements and have a decision scrutinised under the *FWA*. For the rest of the workforce, the discussion must be a lot more about carrot than stick.

The nature of office environments – including open-plan working, constant emails, calls and meetings, leaving at best windows of few minutes at a time without interruption – is such that humans are increasingly reporting an inability to concentrate at their desks. I can attest to tending to take to a quiet cafe when working on a complex piece of work or needing to get the creative juices flowing in the lead-up to a presentation.

According to Cal Newport, bestselling author of *Deep Work*, 'deep work' is 'the ability to focus without distraction on a cognitively demanding task. It's a skill that allows [us] to quickly master complicated information and produce better results in less time'.[91] Newport says deep work makes us better at what we do and provides the sense of true fulfillment that comes from craftsmanship, likening it to a 'superpower' in our increasingly competitive 21st century economy.

Flexible work improves creativity, wellbeing and inclusion, and this is not at the cost of performance, efficiency or profitability. The benefits are win-win.

An OECD study into global 'tele-working' (which we more commonly refer to as remote working; work from home/anywhere; and a form of flexible work arrangement) post-pandemic revealed organisations and humans across the globe can harness the productivity, efficiency and satisfaction gains of flexible working, in the right conditions, including appropriate ICT infrastructure.[92]

The OECD report found that organisational performance, worker satisfaction and efficiency increases with flexible work due to:

- better work-life balance
- less commuting

- fewer distractions leading to more focused work
- less absenteeism.

Conversely, worker satisfaction can also decrease due to:

- solitude
- hidden overtime
- a fusing of private and work life
- an inappropriate working environment at home.

There is improved organisational performance through cost reductions including reduced capital costs (reduced office space and equipment), and reduced labour costs (the pool of workers firms can choose from is enlarged, increasing the skill supply and improving the match between jobs and hires). Hiring costs decrease if higher worker satisfaction reduces voluntary resignations and turnover. Wages may also decrease, particularly where combined with other measures that improve work-life balance such as flexible hours – to the extent workers are willing to give up a higher salary in return for these amenities.[93]

The OECD report cited examples of German establishments that allow for trust-based work practices or self-managed working time (including telework) which demonstrated better product innovation, higher productivity and more intensive worker effort.[94]

To ensure you are forearmed with all the counter arguments you are likely to be presented with as leaders and HR professionals implementing, developing or advocating for flexible work practices and to present an accurate and balance view of the OECD report, note it also identified some of the following challenges or issues:

- Worker efficiency may decrease with reduced in-person interactions, which impairs communication, knowledge flows and managerial oversight – based on the notion that personal meetings allow for more effective communication than more remote forms such as emails, chat or phone calls.
- Less frequent personal communication can also have negative implications for engagements with key stakeholders, such as clients and suppliers, with adverse effects for overall business performance.
- Lack of personal interactions can decrease knowledge flows among employees, given many people learn through interactions with colleagues and may acquire skills through learning by doing.

Somewhat archaically and contrary to everything we are discussing in this book, the OECD report said:

To the extent that control over workers is exerted through face-to-face interactions and physical presence, telework can hinder managerial oversight and aggravate principal-agent problems, e.g. 'shirking', and requires a change from assessing performance in terms of inputs, i.e. time worked, to outputs, which implies giving up some control over workers and, in principle, provides workers with more opportunities to 'slack'.[95]

It further explains, contrary to most of our discussions in this book about trust, flexibility and autonomy that 'digitalisation may also lead to more data on worker performance becoming available to managers, which may ultimately provide more information for efficient monitoring of workers than is generally available in a traditional office environment'.[96]

In Australia we have an interesting evolution of these benefits and concerns raised by leaders against the backdrop of legal compliance under the *FWA*, WHS laws focused on psychosocial hazards, and what is a different operating platform for employers globally. Employees are demanding more trust, autonomy and flexibility in circumstances where it is established flexible working environments drive inclusion, which in turn drives high performance, creativity, engagement and innovation.

While leaders and CEOs have expressed concerns regarding missed mentoring and learning opportunities in the face of flexible working, many employees who started their careers in the midst of statewide lockdowns have also been more reluctant to come into the office, as they realise they are able to perform their roles at home.

These are difficult but important conversations for you to have with your workforce, as leaders and HR professionals. Whatever your policy looks like, it's important you are deliberate about how you engage, particularly with your junior staff, and ensure that mentoring and development occurs. I don't agree that this needs to occur in person or in the office. I accept a lot of communication and learning happens by osmosis in a face-to-face environment and that as leaders we need to be more proactive and deliberate to ensure it continues at home, but there is a lot to be gained from making flexible work arrangements available and it is worth the time and investment to get this right.

As a staunch advocate for flexible working, I am pleased to say mandated office working is just not the way the world is evolving, and that's a good thing.

Flex for equality

It is well accepted that women have historically been responsible for most unpaid care and domestic work. As a result, it has been reported that women are:

- less likely to be employed in a full-time capacity
- more likely to experience discrimination in the workplace
- less likely to have professional development opportunities
- more likely to reduce their working hours
- more likely to take leave
- more likely to change their job or stop work altogether.[97]

As women continue to struggle with the juggle, organisations that promote flexible work for all workers at all levels support them by empowering women to progress. They create an environment where all women are more likely to flourish, thrive or quite frankly (and less ambitiously), manage. Some weeks managing is all women need to aspire to and that is enough.

To reap the benefits of equity and inclusion that flexible working provides, flexibility must be openly and unreservedly available to everyone in the workplace. If we are ever going to achieve gender equity and increase the number of female leaders, executives and board members in our workplaces, they must be enabled in the same way their male counterparts have been for years. If the negative stigma attached to males requesting flexibility and assuming caring and domestic roles is not removed, women will always be at a disadvantage, trying to have it all while they do it all.

The Chief Executive Women and Bain & Company report *The Power of Flexibility* confirmed that 'in order to advance gender equality in the workplace, flexible arrangements must be available to and actively supported for both genders' and that 'where flexible arrangements are widely used, all employees are four times happier'.[98] The report sets out the guidelines listed in Figure 9 to normalise and accelerate the success of flexible working.

FIGURE 9: GUIDELINES FOR NORMALISING AND OPTIMISING FLEXIBLE WORKING

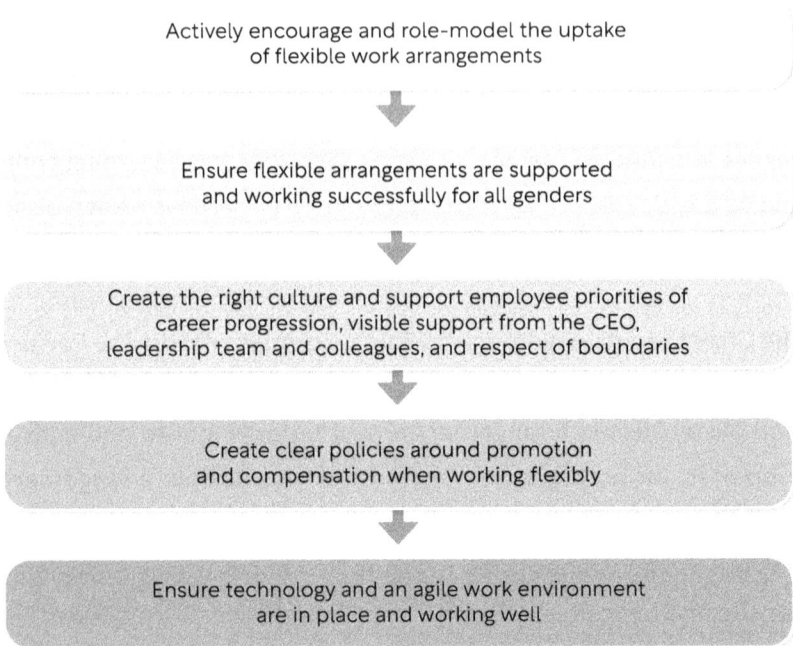

Actively encourage and role-model the uptake of flexible work arrangements

⬇

Ensure flexible arrangements are supported and working successfully for all genders

⬇

Create the right culture and support employee priorities of career progression, visible support from the CEO, leadership team and colleagues, and respect of boundaries

⬇

Create clear policies around promotion and compensation when working flexibly

⬇

Ensure technology and an agile work environment are in place and working well

Adapted from Bain & Company 2016[99]

Unless people of all genders are equally encouraged to access flexible work and share family responsibilities, we will continue to see women struggle with the juggle, with dramatic drops in the progression of women to leadership positions. The stagnation is staggering with 2023 Workplace Gender Equality Agency data revealing:

- a 21.7 per cent gender pay gap across Australia
- only 22 per cent of CEO positions in Australia are held by women
- only 7 per cent of manager roles are part-time.[100]

In her award-winning book *Stop Fixing Women,* Catherine Fox notes that 'women are still far more likely to work part-time in Australia and men who decide to take the flexibility track face a wall of disapproval and career penalties'.[101] She refers to anecdotal material regarding workplaces, particularly in professional services environments, not adjusting to flexibility but instead changing the job status of those who work flexibly by moving them out of client-facing roles. This would not be possible if flexibility became a norm – not only available but regularly used by everyone.

As leaders and HR professionals we need to work on the cultural change required to encourage the take-up of flexible work more broadly. Beyond carers' responsibilities and the impact of flexible work on women when they are raising children, Fox shared some interesting insights about the physical health impacts on women throughout their lifecycle at work in our interview.

The workplace landscape is evolving rapidly, with discussions around women's health, flexible work arrangements and gender bias gaining prominence. Fox says experts are now delving into the health challenges faced by women, particularly during the menopausal transition, shedding light on the economic and workforce implications. The dialogue highlights the critical role of flexible work arrangements in retention, and the persistent biases that hinder women's progress in the professional realm.

A noteworthy issue Fox raised was the impact of menopause on women's retirement. The economic impact of women leaving the workforce years earlier than their male counterparts, often due to menopausal challenges, frames the discussion about menopause as not only as women's health issue but a workforce concern that costs billions worldwide.

Recent research conducted by the Australian Institute of Superannuation Trustees found 45 per cent of women under 55 years were retiring early due to sickness, injury or disability, costing a woman on the average wage more than $500,000 in lost earnings and more than $50,000 in superannuation.[102] AIA Australia found women between the ages of 44 to 55 years were twice as likely to have a mental health claim when compared to men in a similar age bracket. The insurer has launched a project with the Australasian Menopause Society to provide education and tool kits for employers and members to help remove the stigma of menopause, debunk misinformation and manage the condition.[103]

In my conversation with Fox, flexible work arrangements emerged as a potential solution to address the challenges posed by meno-pause. Fox acknowledged that the younger generation of women is increasingly vocal about their expectations regarding work conditions such as working from home. Flexible work, she argued, should not be considered a luxury but a necessary component to retain a diverse ageing workforce. Without flexible options, women might opt to leave the workforce, contributing to a significant loss in talent and expertise and potentially leaving them without financial security in retirement.

Fox also emphasised the biases that still exist around parental leave. While efforts to encourage men to take parental leave were applauded, maternity discrimination remains a reality for many women who get put on the 'mummy track' when returning to jobs. Fox expressed hope that increased male participation in parental leave could lead to a reduction in bias over time. However, she cautioned against overlooking other basic gender biases, with their authority and expertise undervalued or ignored, that contribute to the underrepresentation of women in leadership roles whether they have children or not.

Recognising menopause as a workforce issue is crucial for creating supportive environments that enable women to navigate this phase while continuing their professional journeys. Flexible work, coupled with efforts to address biases comprehensively, is a key strategy for fostering inclusive workplaces that benefit both current and future generations of women in the workforce. As Fox's book revealed, we need to 'stop fixing women' and keep our focus on creating environments that support them.

Tackling flexism and proximity bias

While the transformation the pandemic has brought to workplaces has gone a long way to normalising flexible work and more men are now working from home, several surveys have found a stark gender divide in the rush back to the office. The BBC recently asked if 'male-dominated offices' could be the way of the future, highlighting a UK survey finding 69 per cent of mothers want to work from home at least once a week, compared with 56 per cent of fathers.[104] In Australia, design firm Hassell found in late 2020 that 47 per cent of men want to primarily work in an office, compared with 36 per cent of women.[105]

These findings signal warning signs of proximity bias. While we've long been concerned about 'flexism' – the idea that working flexibly or at home could see people treated differently at work – proximity bias presents a different challenge. Proximity bias is what manifests when some groups of people work in the office while others work at home. It relates to the impact of the additional social interactions those in the office are exposed to, and whether they may get access to better work and thus better results, more promotions and more pay rises.

People will follow their leaders, and if those leaders (who are commonly still white middle-aged men with domestic infrastructure to support them at home) continue to go to the office, their staff will follow. Those who can't or would prefer not to go to the office may be disadvantaged as a result. As more women seem to be capitalising on flexible work in workplaces that were not flexible pre-pandemic, there is concern about the long-term impact of this – particularly if flexible work opportunities are not coupled with a significant cultural shift in the way organisations recognise and reward performance. Unless we are deliberate about this, unintended consequences may follow, and these seemingly positive changes may see women – and others requiring flexible work, such as those with disabilities, chronic health conditions and carer responsibilities – going backwards rather than forwards.

While some men have embraced flexibility and taken on increased carer responsibilities; we have seen many more return to the work-place post-pandemic. If male leaders predominantly work in the office and favour those who are closest to them in the office, what will result from that? These people will be promoted and progress to leadership roles, and the gender pay gap and representation of women and other diverse groups may stagnate or, worse still, plummet.

It is equally important that we tackle flexism faced by men who do embrace flexibility. For men, this scepticism about flexible work is particularly troublesome, given that research from Bain & Company and other sources show that men are twice as likely to have a request for flexible work denied.[106] Data from the Workplace Gender Equality Agency (WGEA) indicates that while 70 per cent of workplaces have a policy and strategy in support of flexible working arrangements, less than 2 per cent have targets for men's take-up of flexible working.[107]

It may be a perception issue that men are not entitled to flexible work arrangements, or antiquated views in relation to who should be caring for children – because these are requests predominantly made to accommodate carer responsibilities.

Even if the request is granted, research by the Australian Human Rights Commission has confirmed that 27 per cent of men who are granted the request are likely to be discriminated against or face an adverse consequence.[108] For example, the men who are accessing flexible work arrangements may be the ones who end up having their roles made redundant, or who are not provided with bonuses, pay increases or adequate promotions when opportunities arise.

It's fair to say these statistics indicate a man's divergence from the socially constructed traditional vocational path have been perceived either as weakness or that the man is not as committed to the workplace as he should be. These are extraordinary and terribly unfair perceptions that negatively impact these men, those they are sharing the caring load with, our workplaces and communities more broadly if left unchecked.

Flex for mental health

Research undertaken by the Diversity Council Australia has also confirmed that flexibility at work positively impacts mental health. Workers who had access to the flexibility they needed to manage work and other commitments were almost four times more likely to feel their work positively impacted their mental health (45 per cent versus 12 per cent).[109]

Unsurprisingly, exclusion was found to negatively impact mental health, with humans who experienced discrimination and/or harassment at work being twice as likely to report their workplace had negatively impacted their mental health (49 per cent), compared to those who had not (21 per cent).

Beyond Blue reports that one in eight men will experience depression and one in five will experience anxiety at some stage in their lives.[110] Flexible work is and should be part of the solution to this. Men who work flexibly experience less stress and burnout and have a higher sense of purpose which makes them healthier.[111]

Diversity Council Australia CEO, Lisa Annese, said organisations need to understand the value of fostering more inclusive and diverse workplaces when it comes to mental health. How we treat humans at work can have a significant impact on their mental health. If humans don't feel valued and respected at work, it can have major knock-on effects on their personal life and mental wellbeing. The data clearly shows that organisations with a strong focus on diversity and inclusion tend to have a positive effect on employee mental health. If you treat people with dignity and respect, have a zero-tolerance approach to bullying and harassment, create flexible workplace environments and have supportive leaders, people flourish.

PwC's 2021 *What Workers Want* report states that 22 per cent of respondents valued employers that support their wellbeing, above all other factors.[112]

Flex for the next generation and an ageing population

The new generation of humans entering our workplaces crave flexibility. Flexible arrangements are not just a nice-to-have, but are strongly linked to engagement and loyalty. It is clear younger workers want both flexibility and job security. It's not about outdated notions of work-life balance that Generation X-ers like me were focused on (and never achieved), but rather work-life integration. They are demanding the right to progress and be rewarded for their efforts (which are increasingly more efficient and productive) and their ability to quickly master new and emerging technology; but equally they require the right to flex and disconnect.

The 12th edition of Deloitte's *Gen Z and Millennial Survey* (which I have followed with interest every year, and now also serves as another reminder of how old I am) released in 2023 confirmed what we already knew anecdotally to be true: the pandemic has prompted humans across the globe to rethink the role work plays in their lives.[113]

The survey found that only 49 per cent of Gen Z respondents say work is central to their identity. They place a strong emphasis on work-life balance, which is the top trait they admire in their peers and a key consideration when they are deciding who to work for. The report emphasised that Gen Z and Millennials deeply value the benefit of flexible work, and crave the freedom to decide not only *where* they work, but also *when* they work.

In a compelling call to leaders to offer or keep offering flexibility for engagement and retention purposes alone, the 2023 survey found that 77 per cent of Gen Z employees and 75 per cent of Millennials who currently work in remote or hybrid roles would consider looking for a new job if their employer asked them to work on site full-time.

Let's take a moment to repeat and unpack that for CEOs calling for a full-time return to the office:

> *More than 75 per cent of your workers currently aged 43 and under will look for work elsewhere if you demand a full-time report to the office.*

Sit with that for a moment.

And it isn't just about attracting and engaging emerging generations. As leaders and HR professionals you also need to consider flexibility to accommodate and retain the ageing population – those at the other end of their lifespan. Humans are working harder for longer. Now more than ever, work is a marathon, not a sprint. Flexible work is the key to endurance in this race. It's the key to retaining talented humans in a highly competitive job market and ensuring your investment in them is capitalised for a longer period. In many cases, people who may be challenged with illness or injury can realise their full potential with small accommodations in where and how they work. They more than often reward organisations who accommodate them with loyalty and longevity.

Mainstreaming flexibility

There is no question that flexible work is a critical enabler in attracting, engaging and retaining diverse groups of humans in the workforce and empowering them to progress to leadership roles. According to Flexible Work Day founder Vanessa Vanderhoek, to tackle flexism, we must let go of stereotypes attached to flexible work as being reserved for 'working mums'.[114] To reap the benefits that flexible or 'agile' work has to offer, Vanessa says 'we must challenge and transform our views about flexible working – in relation to our careers and colleagues, personal and family life, health and wellbeing'.

Diversity Council Australia's Future-Flex initiative focuses on 'mainstreaming flexibility by team design', emphasising the need to move away from ad hoc arrangements for individuals and towards involving their teams to redesign work. Specifically, the guidelines recommend:

- reviewing the components of all team members' jobs (including tasks, duties, responsibilities, location and timing), rather than just one individual employee's
- having employees and managers work together to come up with team-based flexibility solutions, rather than managers doing this in isolation or with just one employee.

Flex for the future

As the saying goes, the more things change, the more they stay the same. While the pandemic created a burning platform for change, we are increasingly seeing some parts of the business community and leaders pushing for a return to the old normal. This is despite the benefits flexibility provided for organisations and humans during the pandemic, and the undeniable upside flexibility delivers in enabling humans to thrive and organisations to prosper.

A survey in October 2023 suggested most chief executives predicted a full return to the office in three years.[115] Atlassian reports that there remain misconceptions about flexible work, and my experience with employers and leaders supports this. Firstly, there is a misconception that humans aren't as productive when they are at home, or that they're working less. Another is that they're less connected to each other in a remote environment, or that an organisation's culture is impossible to replicate in a remote setting, and that executives are not sure how to realise a return on their real estate investment.[116]

The *Lessons Learned: 1,000 Days of Distributed at Atlassian* report describes the results of Atlassian's approach to distributed work. Since 2020, Atlassians have been able to choose where they work, every single day, as part of its Team Anywhere program. The report demonstrated results including a 32 per cent improvement in focus, 31 per cent progress on top priorities and 13 per cent less time in meetings. Further, representation of women had doubled in certain regions, 92 per cent of Atlassian workers said their distributed work policy allows them to do their best work and 91 per cent reported it was an important reason why they stay at Atlassian.[117]

While in-person time can be important for teams, this doesn't need to happen every day; in fact, it can be quite successful even as infrequent team gatherings a few times a year. The report found that more than 80 per cent of workers had visited one of Atlassian's offices at least once each quarter over the previous year. The key is to ensure the face-to-face time teams have is productive and meaningful, to build the connections they need to succeed. Atlassian also promotes setting clear goals and tracking progress rather than rewarding face-time, and gathering key stakeholders for longer, creative brainstorms or facilitating fast, efficient digital discussions rather than defaulting to 30-minute meetings.

Flexible work is the new normal in many workplaces. It is not a nice-to-have, but necessary to attract and engage the next generation of workers, to accommodate the needs of an ageing workforce, to tackle flexism, to reduce burnout, to improve health and wellbeing, to create more inclusive workplaces that close the gender pay gap and see more diverse groups of humans thrive and progress in leadership roles. This can be achieved without a negative impact on productivity, performance or returns to shareholders. Flexibility as the norm provides the structural foundation to build diverse and inclusive workplaces that organisations and our society reaps the benefits of. To that end, flexible work benefits everyone.

Inclusion at work

Inclusion is not a buzzword, it's a way of life. It's not something we switch on and off when it suits us – when we want to win an award, pitch for a tender or achieve a benchmark or accreditation. It's a conscious choice we make in the way we show up every day for the benefit of humans in our workplace, our organisation and our society.

Since 2017 Diversity Council Australia has been quantifying and publishing reports on the benefits of inclusion in its annual Inclusion@Work Index.[118] Diversity in the context of the index includes the attributes visualised in Figure 10.

FIGURE 10: DIVERSITY ATTRIBUTES

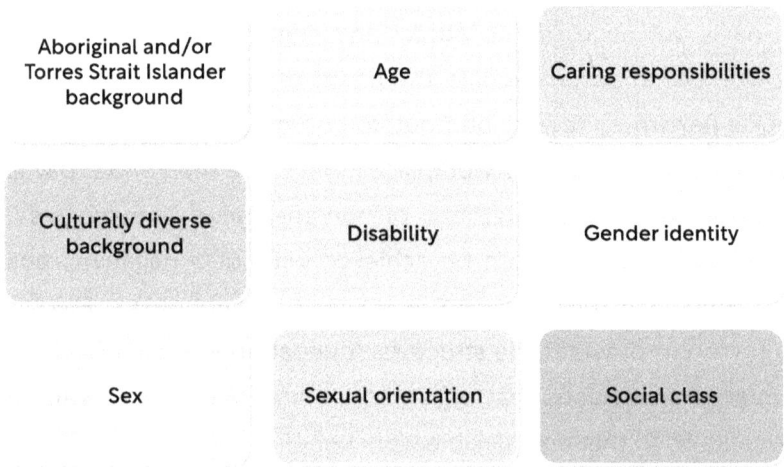

Aboriginal and/or Torres Strait Islander background	Age	Caring responsibilities
Culturally diverse background	Disability	Gender identity
Sex	Sexual orientation	Social class

The Inclusion@Work Index considers inclusion across four pillars to measure whether diverse humans in an organisation are:

1. **RESPECTED:** feel valued and respected for who they are.

2. **CONNECTED:** feel connected to their co-workers and feel they belong.

3. **PROGRESSING:** have opportunities to develop their career and progress.

4. **CONTRIBUTING:** can contribute their talents to the organisation.[119]

Humans across the country are craving an inclusive workplace with the latest Inclusion@Work Index confirming three out of four Australian workers support or strongly support their organisation taking action to create a workplace that is diverse and inclusive.[120]

Year after year, the results have consistently proven the incredible benefits inclusion brings. The 2023–2024 Inclusion@Work Index confirms again that workplace inclusion significantly increases performance and wellbeing and decreases discrimination and harassment. People working in inclusive teams are:

- 10 times more likely to be **very satisfied**
- 9.5 times more likely to be **innovative**
- 8.5 times more likely to **work effectively together**
- 4 times more likely to provide **excellent customer service**
- 4 times more likely to feel work has a **positive impact on their mental health**
- 2.5 times more likely to be willing to **work extra hard** to help the team success

- 2.5 times more likely to have been **given feedback they found useful**
- 5 times less likely to **experience discrimination and/or harassment at work**
- 3 times less likely to **leave the organisation**.[121]

This echoes what I have been saying to leaders for many years. Creating inclusive workplaces decreases compliance risks and legal claims. It's the high watermark and will often also manifest in baseline compliance (although policies and procedures still need to be in place to deal with the exceptions when humans go rogue).

Leaders make or break diversity and inclusion initiatives in the workplace. It doesn't matter how many targets an organisation sets or what it says about diversity and inclusion on its website, leaders hold the key to whether an organisation is truly inclusive.

To be an inclusive leader you must create an inclusive team environment, value difference, seek out and use diverse ideas, treat everyone fairly and deal with inappropriate behaviour.[122]

According to diversity and inclusion experts, Juliet Bourke and Andrea Titus, what leaders say and do makes up to a 70 per cent difference as to whether humans feel included. They identified signature traits of inclusive leaders depicted in Figure 11.[123]

FIGURE 11: SIGNATURE TRAITS OF INCLUSIVE LEADERS

Adapted from Bourke and Titus 2020[124]

Being an inclusive leader is about so much more than what you say you will do. While a visible commitment is critical, it's also about how this is reflected in the way you show up and lead every day.

In my interview with Exsona founder Ryan McGrory, he offered the following insights about what makes up a diverse, equitable and inclusive workplace culture:

1. A place where people feel they belong.

2. A culture that values diverse perspectives.

3. A culture that's fair.

McGrory posited while may leaders 'talk the talk' when it comes to inclusion they lean too heavily on optics, not reality. McGrory said organisations that 'walk the walk' reap the greater benefits diversity and inclusion brings, including for innovation. He identified the following three actions to achieve an inclusive culture:

1. **GIVE YOUR PEOPLE A VOICE AND LISTEN WELL.** Be a conscious listener and make an ongoing effort to gain perspectives, feedback and ideas from your people and act by removing barriers and enabling improvements.

2. **BE INTENTIONAL.** Have a diversity, equity and inclusion strategy that is not just a calendar full of dress-up days and morning teas. A strategy with objectives, targets, actions, a solid communication plan, and a roadmap that guides it.

3. **LINK YOUR DIVERSITY, EQUITY AND INCLUSION STRATEGY TO YOUR ORGANISATION STRATEGY.** Understand the organisation's vision and objectives and use this information to inform and influence the creation of the diversity, equity and inclusion strategy.

McGrory says these three things work together and should be singing in unison – your listening strategy, your diversity, equity and inclusion strategy and your organisation strategy help create a culture that listens well, acts, collaborates effectively, shares ideas, drives innovation and improves the lives of the people and performance of the organisation. As a leader, make a genuine commitment to get behind the strategy, embrace it, lead by example and allow your actions and behaviours to set the tone for the entire organisation.

Social class

I have talked a lot about gender in this book, which mirrors society generally when we consider diversity, equity and inclusion initiatives. However, as leaders and HR professionals we need to consider and address intersectional issues that impact the experience, inclusion or exclusion of humans in our workplace. For this purpose I spoke to Lisa Annese, CEO of Diversity Council Australia, about the important inclusion initiatives often missing or underemphasised in Australian workplaces.

Class at work is something that has always struck me as being pivotal to inclusion, but very little is written about it. I have personally experienced class-based exclusion at work. In a performance review in my first year as a qualified lawyer, I expressed my interest in attending a public speaking course. The private-school-educated elite leader I reported to suggested in writing in response to my learning and development request that an elocution course would be a more appropriate place to start. I promptly looked up 'elocution' as I had not heard of the term before. Elocution is the skill of clear speech, distinct pronunciation and articulation. In other words, they wanted me to speak 'proper'. Less western Sydney perhaps? They didn't go so far as to suggest this, but might as well have. Message received.

In a first-in-class study, Diversity Council Australia partnered with Suncorp and Novartis to undertake a survey of more than 3000 workers to see if social class makes a difference in the land of the 'fair go'. The study revealed that class, more than any other diversity demographic investigated in the Inclusion@Work Index, is the most strongly linked to workers' experience of inclusion and one of the most strongly linked to exclusion.[125]

The results of the survey were fascinating, albeit not at all surprising to me. The study also found that:

- 43 per cent of lower-class workers had personally experienced discrimination and/or harassment in the workplace in the previous 12 months, compared to 26 per cent of higher-class workers
- lower-class workers were more likely to be ignored (17 per cent) compared to middle-class workers (6 per cent) and higher-class workers (7 per cent)
- lower-class workers were more likely to miss out on opportunities and privileges (22 per cent) compared to middle-class workers (9 per cent) and higher-class workers (9 per cent)
- lower-class workers were more likely to be left out of social gatherings (20 per cent) compared to middle-class workers (6 per cent) and higher-class workers (7 per cent).[126]

In our interview, Annese shared the following with me:

We have this narrative that class doesn't matter in Australia, but when we ask, 'What social class did you grow up in?', everyone can answer. Our beliefs are based on our colonial past – we didn't import the British formal aristocracy into Australia. We don't have lords and ladies. We don't have that kind of aristocracy, even though we still are part of the Commonwealth and our head of state is the King.

But we imported a lot of the culture, especially the private school/public school divide, and anyone who's done research on social cohesion and opportunity knows social class plays a big role. The diversity inclusion movement in Australia came out of the women's movement. That's why it looks different to the UK, where social class is part of it. It looks different to the US, which came out of civil rights in the US, so it's mainly about race. History matters.

Diversity Council Australia's research clearly shows that, more than any other aspect of identity, social class impacts inclusion at work – more than race, gender or sex, sexuality, disability and even being a First Nations Australian. Annese said:

If you're from the wrong side of the tracks, or you've grown up very working class, there are more barriers.

Class may not be top of mind when we talk about inclusion at work, but these early insights clearly reveal that it should be. Annese told me that movable things such as socioeconomic status, job and income can change, there are unmovable factors – such as family of origin, schooling and connections – that affect inclusion. This is why people with no income can be from a high social class – because of their connections.

Dr Terry Fitzsimmons at the University of Queensland studied the childhood attributes of the top 200 ASX leaders in Australia.[127] His work provides insights that are important to appreciate when considering whether to incorporate class into your diversity, equity and inclusion strategies. His study demonstrates the many intersectional considerations to consider. Our history and personal circumstances matter; they shape us humans and leaders. Some insights from Fitzsimmons' study are presented in Figure 12.

FIGURE 12: COMMON ATTRIBUTES OF THE TOP 200 ASX LEADERS

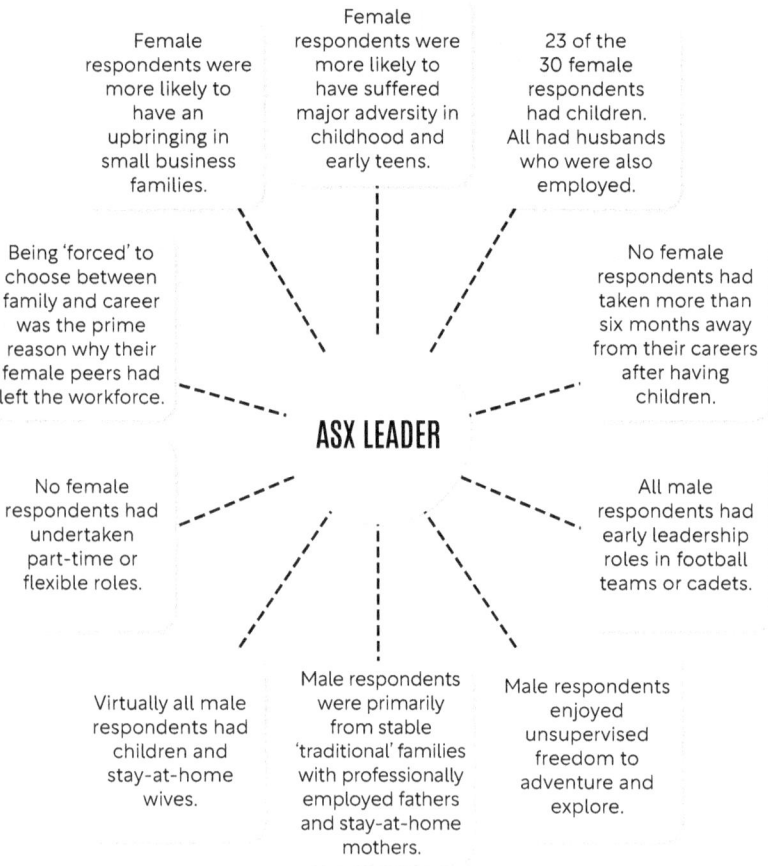

Female respondents were more likely to have an upbringing in small business families.

Female respondents were more likely to have suffered major adversity in childhood and early teens.

23 of the 30 female respondents had children. All had husbands who were also employed.

Being 'forced' to choose between family and career was the prime reason why their female peers had left the workforce.

No female respondents had taken more than six months away from their careers after having children.

ASX LEADER

No female respondents had undertaken part-time or flexible roles.

All male respondents had early leadership roles in football teams or cadets.

Virtually all male respondents had children and stay-at-home wives.

Male respondents were primarily from stable 'traditional' families with professionally employed fathers and stay-at-home mothers.

Male respondents enjoyed unsupervised freedom to adventure and explore.

Adapted from Fitzsimmons 2011[128]

As I reviewed these attributes, it was illuminating to realise I shared all the attributes of the female respondents.

Drawing on this research, Annese said a key defining characteristic that propelled women into leadership was adversity early in life. Annese noted that when we bring social class into the conversation, we recognise humans who have not traditionally been part of the conversation on inclusion. We recognise they lack privilege as well:

> Men are constantly told if you're a straight white man you rule the world. But if you're a straight white man who's doing dangerous dirty work, or you're in the gig economy, you are not coming from the position of privilege that is usually associated with your gender and race.

We must recognise social class to engage people who lack this privilege. Diversity Council Australia research showed that men from lower social classes are not engaged with diversity equity and inclusion. A focus on social class as an attribute could change this.

Cultural and racial marginalisation

Cultural diversity and inclusion is another important focus for leaders and HR professionals. We need to have more metrics and initiatives focusing on this. What we measure matters and is often prioritised to get done. We need to focus on culture and race as a key pillar of inclusion but also on the double jeopardy it creates for women from an intersectional perspective which of course multiplies and perpetuates depending on further attributes that also exist (eg. social class, sexuality and disability).

In our discussion, Annese recommended we should pivot from the use of the term 'culturally and linguistically diverse' (CALD) to 'culturally and racially marginalised' (CARM). Annese said this term recognises that racism is rooted in a social process called racialisation. This is where some groups come to be viewed as different, 'outside the norm' and/or 'inferior' due to their race, ethnicity, language or religion and, based on those perceptions, they receive unequal treatment. Racialisation creates a society in which some groups are racially privileged, while others are racially marginalised. Racialisation happens in response to people's arbitrary physical characteristics (for example skin colour, hair texture and facial features), as well as accent, language, name, religion and clothing.[129]

Diversity Council Australia research shows the experience of people who experience exclusion has very little to do with the language they speak. It is based on visible physical phenotype and religious stress. In today's increasingly diverse workplaces, discussions around diversity and inclusion have become more nuanced, revealing the complexities of individuals' experiences.

Annese highlighted a significant flaw in the term CALD: it groups together individuals from vastly different cultural and racial backgrounds. A woman from Sweden and a woman from Pakistan, for instance, may share the CALD label, but their experiences at work can be drastically different. The term CALD overlooks the unique challenges and privileges associated with each racial group, leading to an inadequate understanding of workplace dynamics.

Annese challenged the notion of racial neutrality, asserting that humans are either racially privileged or marginalised. If someone must consistently think about their race, they fall into the racially marginalised category. If they don't, they are racially privileged. This perspective challenges the common belief that some individuals are immune to racial biases, emphasising the need for a deeper understanding of privilege and marginalisation.

It is clear the experiences of racism are dynamic and change over time. Ancestry alone does not determine one's experience of racial exclusion. Annese says who is racially marginalised or privileged depends on the distribution of power at a given time. Drawing again on our history, Annese explained culture and language is relevant to this discussion. However, she emphasised the need to shift the focus to race. She advocates for building racial literacy among members to foster a deeper understanding of the racial dynamics at play in the workplace:

Race-based terms were removed from our language in the 1970s. We were ashamed of the White Australia policy. We moved to the language of non-English speaking background. We sanitised. We don't talk about the International Day of the Elimination of Racial Discrimination. We talk about harmony.

The issue for CARM people isn't whether people like their food or their clothes. The problem is that if you're a woman who looks Asian, you're assumed to be more submissive. You might be fetishised such that sexual harassment looks different if you're an Asian woman; or if you're a woman who wears a headdress, it may be assumed you're oppressed. This is about racial phenotype and markers of a visible difference and that's what we want to focus on.

The interview with Annese challenged the prevailing narrative around diversity and inclusion, urging a shift from broad labels such as CALD to a more nuanced understanding of racial dynamics. By fostering racial literacy and acknowledging the dynamic nature of racism, leaders can create more inclusive workplaces where individuals are recognised and valued for their unique experiences rather than being grouped within generic categories. It's a call to action for leaders to move beyond superficial discussions of culture and language and engage in meaningful dialogues about race and its impact on the workplace.

Belonging

Belonging is where the true magic of diversity and inclusion comes to life. Belonging occurs when humans with diverse attributes are included, their contribution is valued, and they feel they can share their true and authentic selves with other humans in the workplace. As inclusion strategist Verna Myers said, 'diversity is being invited to the party; inclusion is being asked to dance.' Belonging is when humans dance like noone is watching. Therein lies the beauty of being safe at work.

Humans have an innate need to belong – to one another, to our friends and families, to our culture, organisation and society. When people feel like they belong at work, they are more productive, motivated, engaged and 3.5 times more likely to contribute to their fullest potential.[130]

When humans feel they belong, they and their organisations reap the benefits. Figure 13 shows some of the benefits of belonging according to a study reported in *Harvard Business Review.*[131]

FIGURE 13: THE VALUE OF BELONGING

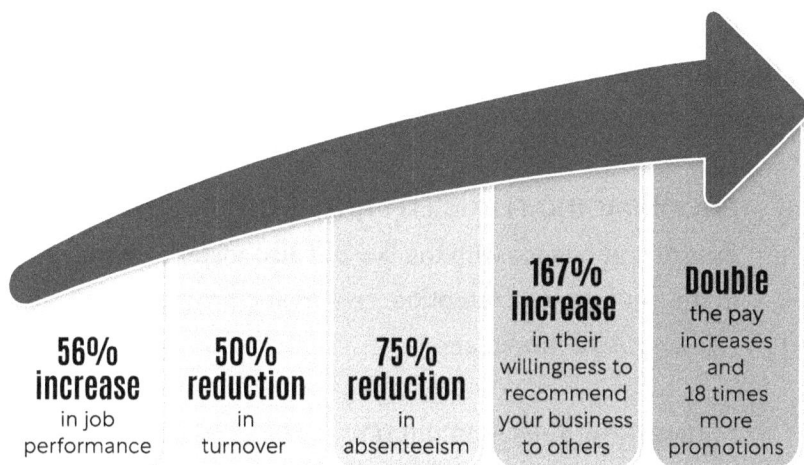

56% increase
in job performance

50% reduction
in turnover

75% reduction
in absenteeism

167% increase
in their willingness to recommend your business to others

Double the pay increases and 18 times more promotions

Adapted from Carr et al. 2019[132]

To achieve belonging, you must communicate with the people in your workplace to understand what they need. You need compassionate leaders who are vulnerable and lead with empathy. You need allies in the workplace for diverse groups to engage with each other and celebrate the benefits diversity brings. You need to build workplaces where humans feel safe to bring their true and authentic selves to work without fear of being ridiculed or excluded. You need humans to connect with their purpose and feel the unique gifts and differences they bring are an important and valuable contribution to achieving the team's and organisation's objectives. You need humans to know that if they dance like no-one is watching, they will be celebrated, embraced and encouraged to thrive. That is the beauty and bliss of inclusion and belonging. It is the key to thriving humans, leaders and organisations. As Audre Lorde said, 'It is not our differences that divide us. It is our inability to recognize, accept, and celebrate those differences.'

Key actions

As leaders and HR professionals, you can empower humans to flourish and thrive at work by fostering an environment conducive to flexibility and inclusion by:

○ **ENCOURAGING FLEXIBILITY AND INCLUSION** to not only ensure compliance with the law but also fostering equity in the engagement, retention, reward and progression of all humans in the workplace.

○ **MAINSTREAMING FLEXIBILITY** – whilst diverse groups including carers, women, older workers and those living with disability, illness or injury are more likely to thrive in flexible workplaces, flexibility is most effective when it is mainstreamed and available to everyone in the workplace indiscriminately.

○ **PROMOTING THE BUSINESS BENEFITS OF INCLUSION** – cultivating inclusive workplaces leads to greater employee satisfaction, innovation, collaboration, and enhanced customer service. When humans feel included and valued, they contribute to not only safer but more successful organisations.

○ **ASPIRING TO CREATE ENVIRONMENTS WHERE EVERY HUMAN FEELS A SENSE OF BELONGING** as this is where the magic happens. This is when humans are truly safe.

Chapter 10

Enforce policies and exit jerks

You have seen throughout this book the damage that toxic people and behaviours can wreak on your workplace. Netflix founder Reed Hastings said, 'Do not tolerate brilliant jerks. The cost to teamwork is too high.' The damage extends well beyond teamwork, though. It affects culture, productivity, reputation and brand, and exponentially increases legal risk for the organisation and the leaders who tolerate the behaviour. It also destroys humans.

We've established that toxic workplaces impose serious and lasting harm on affected people. You have learnt in this book that humans who are exposed to a toxic culture are likely to suffer from greater stress, anxiety, depression and burnout, and are more likely to be diagnosed with a serious physical disease. This not only increases legal liability but destroys the very fabric of the positive workplace cultures leaders must create to ensure the safety of humans in the workplace and the performance and profitability of the organisation.

Organisational psychologist Tomas Chamorro-Premuzic does not mince his words about the impact toxic leaders can have on organisations and humans working in them:

> Incompetent [leaders] result in anxious, alienated workers who practice counterproductive work behaviours and spread toxicity ... Instead of promoting people based on their charisma, overconfidence, and narcissism, we must put in charge people with actual competence, humility, and integrity.[133]

Similarly, management experts Sull and Sull found that leadership consistently emerged as the best predictor of toxic culture. They said:

> Managers reinforce or undermine through their actions, and entrenched social norms influence who is promoted to leadership positions ... Toxic social norms can take on a life of their own in a team or an organisation and persist through multiple changes in leadership.[134]

They concluded leaders must model the behaviour they expect from employees. Humans look to leaders for guidance on culture, but they tend to discount lofty statements about abstract values. They closely observe what leaders do for signals about what behaviour is encouraged, expected and tolerated.[135]

The findings support what I have observed in practice: leaders are twice as important as company-level policies in terms of whether an employee with a track record of misconduct is promoted or fired. Not dealing with unethical employees comes at a high cost, and employees who have committed misconduct are more likely to do so in the future.[136]

For years I have been tirelessly advising organisations and leaders that dysfunction perpetuates. It's critical you pick up the small breaches of policies and procedures, departures from values and inappropriate workplace behaviours. If left unchecked, from little things big things grow. Dysfunction is a slippery slope and the further leaders let it slide, the harder it becomes to rein it in.

Promoting jerks, no matter how technically or financially brilliant management thinks they are, can foster cutthroat subcultures that hurt the bottom line. Organisations too often make promotion decisions based on performance as an individual contributor rather than on a human's ability to create a healthy subculture.[137] Nothing will kill a great employee faster than watching you tolerate a bad one.[138]

Toxic social norms increase the odds that even good people will behave poorly, as they act at the group level rather than the individual level. Humans follow social norms because other humans do the same. Any improvement of social norms, therefore, requires a coordinated change in expectations and behaviour for the group, rather than one or two team members making unilateral changes.[139]

If, as a leader, you are serious about building safe, healthy, respectful and inclusive workplace cultures, you simply cannot tolerate the intolerable. You must be prepared to get rid of jerks who perpetuate dysfunction no matter how much value you think they seem to add to your top line. If you don't, they will destroy your workplace, break humans in it and, ultimately, that *will* have a much more detrimental impact on your bottom line.

The tide has well and truly turned. It is now more critical than ever that policies are consistently and indiscriminately enforced, no matter who the perpetrator is and regardless of their perceived 'value' to the organisation.

The cost to the organisation of inappropriate, unhealthy and disrespectful behaviours will always outweigh any top-line benefit a perpetrator is perceived to bring.

The cost to health and safety is far too high as inaction or paltry consequences in lieu of serious discipline is a serious impediment to the creation of safe, healthy and inclusive workplaces.

The physical, psychological and economic impact of failing to act is catastrophic for humans in your workplace. The culture of your organisation will be shaped by the worst behaviour you, as the leader, are prepared to tolerate.[140] You can no longer tolerate jerks who create toxic workplace cultures and perpetrate unlawful conduct including bullying and sexual harassment, no matter how brilliant they try to convince you they are.

You must have an effective process for addressing and resolving worker complaints. Humans in your workplace should know how to, and feel comfortable to, raise concerns and sound the alarm. Where humans feel they cannot speak up, or that they won't be taken seriously if they do, your workplace culture and values will be undermined, and dysfunction will result.

Policies and procedures are only effective if backed by a safe and inclusive workplace culture underpinned by values such as inclusion, respect and trust. Policies and procedures quickly become ineffective when they are not promulgated to ensure consistent and indiscriminate enforcement. I said it before and I will say it again: your culture will eat compliance for breakfast.

Key actions

We have covered a lot of material in this book, and I have given you plenty of tangible actions and takeouts to follow. At this point, I encourage you to stop and actively reflect; to hold the mirror up to reflect on the leader you have been, and consider the leader you would like to be.

○ **IS THERE A TIME IN YOUR CAREER THAT YOU FELL SHORT** of the standards and expectations of leaders discussed in this chapter?

○ **WHY DID THIS OCCUR?** What was standing in the way of you acting as you think you should have, or wish you had?

○ If the same thing happened tomorrow, **WHAT WOULD YOU DO DIFFERENTLY?**

Chapter 11

Bringing it all together

It's time to bring everything we have learnt in this book together by working through a potential scenario you could be faced with in your work.

Imagine you've just landed your dream job as CEO of Dream Co Pty Ltd. The organisation has recently developed an app that is set to take the world by storm. You left a stable and secure job as an executive to take this opportunity and are determined to make it work.

Harry was the brains behind the app, but the intellectual property is owned by Dream Co. When the chair of the board approached you about the role, he explained that Harry has been managing the business, but the board feels he is not the right person to take the organisation to the next level as it moves towards listing on the Australian Stock Exchange. You have been offered significant incentives and the opportunity to take up shares in Dream Co if you are successful in getting the business listed. This will make all the financial difference for your family of five as you have just taken on a big mortgage that you are struggling to service with rising interest rates.

In your first three months at work, you meet with each member of the executive team one on one. You run focus groups with the staff to get to know them better, and work through the vision, values and objectives to develop your strategy to present to the board. It becomes apparent that the other executive team members really don't like Harry. Quite a few of them make comments to you 'off the record' that 'he has form'; that 'he can do no wrong'; that he is a 'protected species'.

During the focus groups with staff, you become concerned. They say very little and nothing of substance. They seem nervous, agree with everything you say and don't volunteer any answers unless prompted, and even then, they are very agreeable and bereft. When you approach some employees that you feel you have built rapport with to get insight to what may be happening, they simply respond with, 'I really need this job. I don't want to get involved,' which you find troubling.

You review the workforce planning data and realise the business operates with a running 20 per cent vacancy rate on operational roles, which you are concerned will be putting strain on existing employees in an already demanding and past-faced environment. You also observe that several employees have left within 12 months of commencing in their role and there have been no exit interviews undertaken. There is no further information freely available to you about the reason for the many resignations.

When you ask if anyone works part-time or flexibly, the office manager who looks after HR in her portfolio is quick to advise you, 'That's not possible here.' She clarifies that Harry likes people close by so he can see what they are doing and ensure they are available to do urgent work when he needs them to. When you ask IT about technological capability and security for remote working you are reassured that all devices are indeed portable, and staff could theoretically work from anywhere productively and securely, but again it's reinforced that 'Harry prefers people to be in the office.'

The executive team is a homogenous group of white, middle-aged cisgender men. Before you joined, the Dream Co board worked with Harry to hire Sally, who is expected to progress to executive leadership in 12 months. She was hired to ensure there was another person to work on the app with Harry. Sally is 32-year-old up-and-comer in technology who has received many awards for her achievements, having come to Australia as a refugee when she was 16. She was previously the Chief Technology Officer of a much larger organisation and has a growing online profile with many followers that Dream Co can leverage to market the app. Sally has two young children and often rushes out of the office just after 5pm to make daycare pick-up. You notice she logs on after hours and frequently works to midnight.

Two months into your role, Harry approaches you and says things 'aren't working out' with Sally, and he has decided he will not be confirming her employment after the six-month probation period. He says she is not committed to the business like the other executive members and he doesn't believe she has 'what it takes' to get there. Harry says he is concerned about her delivery which he describes as chaotic and judgements which he says are 'too emotional'. He says now that you are CEO, he no longer needs to discuss this decision with the board as it's an operational decision and none of their business.

You are not comfortable with this and decide to have a 'check-in' meeting with Sally to see how she is going. Sally tells you she has never felt so broken and defeated as she has been in the last five months in her role. She says Harry has taken issue with everything she has done, undermined her to the team, board and other stakeholders, taken credit for work she has done, not let her speak in management meetings and directed her not to discuss anything with you or the board. She says she cannot sleep or eat and has seen a doctor and commenced taking medication for post-traumatic stress symptoms. She adds that Harry tried to kiss her in a taxi after a business dinner recently. She says things were always bad with Harry but now they are unbearable as he has been worse to her since she rejected his advances.

She tells you she did not make a complaint as she was worried she would lose her job and she really needs it to support her family. She also says she owes it to the community of women in tech she represents to stand up to people like Harry and that she is also worried for many of the staff who are also 'broken' by Harry's behaviour towards them. She says, through tears, 'If he has managed to break me as a leader in tech in just five short months, imagine the impact he has had on them over the years.'

You ask the office manager where you can find the policies and procedures in relation to appropriate behaviour in the workplace, and she tells you there aren't any as Harry's view is they 'create problems'.

What do you do?

Start with baseline compliance

Consult with staff and undertake a comprehensive risk assessment of psychosocial hazards in the workplace.

Run targeted and specific surveys and focus groups to understand the risks that exist including in relation to working conditions, behaviours and psychological safety in the workplace. Given the extent of fear and lack of trust you have identified in the workplace, you may need to bring in an impartial consultant such as an organisational psychologist to assist with these discussions with employees or to coach you on strategies to build trust in your conversations with them.

Set up an employee assistance program for staff. Reassure them it is safe to speak up and that you are working on making the workplace culture better and safer for everyone.

Implement policies and procedures in relation to:

- WHS including consultation and risk management on psychosocial hazards
- bullying
- discrimination
- sexual harassment and other unlawful conduct under the Respect@Work laws
- complaints resolution (including investigations and trauma informed management of complaints)
- flexible working, to, as a minimum, ensure compliance with the National Employment Standards for employees entitled to flexibility under the *FWA*.

Align with purpose, values and trust

Work with employees to develop Dream Co's purpose and values. Make the process meaningful, collaborate and inspire them with the vision you have for the future.

Agree on the behaviours you expect from each other and make it clear you will not tolerate behaviour that deviates from these values.

Communicate openly and honestly with employees and help them understand the impact on Dream Co's culture, performance and people if the intolerable is tolerated.

Encourage bystander action. You need to break down the barriers and fear that has built over a long period. You need to rebuild trust in Dream Co and the team and build faith in your leadership. You need to give employees hope that they will have a brighter future under your leadership. This will take time. Reassure your people that they are safe if they speak up, explaining that you can more effectively help them if they do. Help them see that the standard they walk past is the standard they accept and that when they bring things to you, you will listen, act and not tolerate the unlawful, toxic and dysfunctional behaviours that deviate from Dream Co's values and the standards of behaviour that have been set and communicated.

Flourish with flexibility and inclusion

Beyond compliance with *FWA* flexible working entitlements, implement flexible working initiatives to:

- Attract and retain staff – given the 20 per cent vacancy rate and high turnover of staff, flexibility will help you attract and retain diverse employees including women, older workers and those with disabilities and carers responsibilities. Ensure they are set up for success so their pay and opportunities will not be adversely affected, and they can progress into leadership roles.
- Manage psychosocial hazards in the workplace by assisting employees to achieve better work-life balance and attract and retain more people to help take the workload burden from the existing employees, reducing the risk of burnout and associated claims.
- Develop a more inclusive workplace culture to improve organisational performance, productivity, efficiency, customer service and in turn returns to shareholders.

Enforce policies and exit jerks

It's time for Harry to go. He can no longer be a protected species. You will need to consider his contractual provisions and your legal obligations to manage this, but it is clear he is a liability for Dream Co and has put humans and the organisation at significant risk.

Option 1

If Harry is paid *under* the high-income threshold under the *FWA* or covered by an award or enterprise agreement, he will be able to bring an unfair dismissal claim.

On this basis an investigation should be undertaken into the sexual harassment allegations. Given the seriousness of the allegations, Harry's seniority and the risks to Dream Co, this should ideally be outsourced and commissioned under legal professional privilege (to try to avoid the risks to the organisation of the report being provided to a regulator or court if a legal claim is made). The organisation may choose to waive privilege over the report at a later stage or it may be challenged but it is best to set this up at the outset and deal with objections as they arise (with the benefit of legal advice).

If the findings are substantiated, a disciplinary process should be followed including putting the allegations to Harry and asking him to show cause why Dream Co should not proceed with the summary termination of his employment (without notice) for serious misconduct.

OR:

Option 2

If Harry is paid over the high-income threshold under the *FWA* and not covered by an award or enterprise agreement, he will not be able to bring an unfair dismissal claim. In these circumstances Dream Co may decide to terminate his employment without following the process above but instead on notice, without cause (being a standard provision in executive agreement albeit with longer notice periods) given you have lost trust and confidence in his leadership, regardless of the outcome of any investigation. While Harry should not 'serve out' his notice period on site in these circumstances, Dream Co may either pay him in lieu of notice or direct him to take garden leave.

This will mean Harry will not have access to the office, customers and staff while he serves out his notice period but he will be required to provide any information or support required during the handover period including passwords, client information and so on and will not be able to work for another employer during this period or set up a competitor business.

While this may be an easier way out, option one may be preferred if Dream Co:

1. does not want to provide Harry with notice or pay in lieu the circumstances. That is, if the allegations of sexual harassment are investigated and substantiated, Dream Co can terminate Harry's employment for serious misconduct without notice or payment in lieu (which in senior executive contracts tends to be between three to six months – i.e. a significant amount to pay someone who may be guilty of serious misconduct). Sometimes an investigation is commenced and then a deal is done for something short of the full notice period but this would usually come with a non-disparagement clause that would prevent Dream Co from saying anything disparaging about Harry and his conduct which may not be ideal in the circumstances, particularly if the matter leaks to the media and Dream Co wants to respond.

2. may want to communicate to employees and key stake-holders that Harry's employment was terminated for serious misconduct. An independent investigation allows Dream Co to indicate findings were made that it acted on to terminate Harry's employment. Caution should be exercised in doing so

to not waive privilege under any legally privileged investigation and report and minimise risks and exposures to a defamation claim. Again, legal advice is strongly recommended before any statements are made.

Moving forward

Sally and the team around her need to be set up for success. Harry should be directed to undertake an appropriate handover and business protection strategies should be deployed to manage intellectual property, confidential information and investor and customer relationships.

The message should be delivered to your people loud and clear: the culture of Dream Co has changed, and you will no longer tolerate unlawful, toxic or dysfunctional behaviours on your watch.

(As an aside, don't call Harry a jerk in public. That could be a legal risk, too.)

FINAL THOUGHTS

The common thread throughout this book is that a broken workplace is one underpinned by *fear*. Where fear is present, humans in your workplace are not safe, which increases legal risk and liability and adversely impacts organisational performance and your success as a leader.

When humans are safe at work, they *trust* you. This not only reduces legal risk and liability but increases organisational performance and empowers you to create a safe, healthy, respectful and inclusive workplace where humans thrive on your watch.

As a leader, your most fundamental job – not only minimise legal claims but to ensure the success of your organisation and the humans in it – is to tip the scale in favour of trust to ensure humans are safe at work (see Figure 14).

FIGURE 14: BROKEN VERSUS SAFE AT WORK

SAFE

Humans provided with flexibility, autonomy and adopt a growth mindset. They trust they can show vulnerability about personal and professional challenges and that leaders will support them.

Humans trust they can safely speak up about unlawful conduct and that leaders will protect them when they do.

Humans trust they belong and will be respected, included and feel safe to bring their whole self to work.

TRUST

BROKEN

Fear of making mistakes, showing vulnerability, asking for flexibility or disconnecting from work leading to uncertainty, insecurity and burnout.

Fear of bullying, sexual harassment and other unlawful conduct.

Fear of speaking up about unlawful conduct without being subjected to victimisation and adverse consequences.

FEAR

#NotOnMyWatch

Before the Respect@Work laws commenced, I called for leaders in organisations across Australia to step up and take a stand against sexual harassment in their workplace using the hashtag #NotOnMyWatch.

Having seen the catastrophic impact of bullying, sexual harassment and toxic dysfunctional cultures, I asked that leaders in any organisation, large or small, make a public statement that they will not tolerate this behaviour on their watch. It's a simple ask; indeed, it's a requirement that has been mandated by law for 40 years. It's a requirement that most organisations and leaders commit to in their very own policies and procedures. Yet publicly, silence. Crickets. Why?

I tend to swing from cynic to utopian. When you look behind the curtain, as I do every day in my work, the challenges of managing fallible humans are understandable. But enough is enough.

It is now a requirement to discharge your obligations under WHS and the Respect@Work laws.[141] As a leader, you must commit to:

- not shrugging off or walking past anything that constitutes bullying, sexual harassment or other unlawful conduct in the workplace
- speaking up against and addressing bullying, sexual harassment or other unlawful conduct that occurs on your watch
- investigating and, if bullying, sexual harassment or other unlawful conduct is substantiated, disciplining and exiting jerks, regardless of their clients, relationships, public profile, revenue generation, technical skills, perceived brilliance or commercial value.

Using this hashtag does not mean that your conduct as a leader or bystander or the culture of your workplace has always been beyond reproach. Rather, it's a commitment to not tolerate the intolerable.

You can't fix the past. You can't fix what's been done or not been done before. You can't rewrite history or the standards you have walked past before. The time has, however, come to take a stand. To make a change.

You must stand up and make a positive statement about what you commit to and won't tolerate on your watch. Silence allows the failings of our system, toxic workplace cultures, bullying, sexual harassment, other unlawful conduct and, in turn, dysfunction to perpetuate. This can't be the standard you are prepared to walk past. This can't be what we want for our country, for our workplaces, our teams, our humans, our children.

The time has come to say #NotOnMyWatch to unlawful conduct including bullying and sexual harassment in the workplace. #NotOnMyWatch due to the increased risks, damages, penalties and personal culpability. #NotOnMyWatch due the public outcry against offenders and the destructive brand damage it causes. #NotOnMyWatch due to staff turnover, absenteeism, lost productivity and other hard costs arising from it. #NotOnMyWatch not only because of the impact on your bottom line but the devastating impact on the health and safety of humans in your workplace. #NotOnMyWatch because it's time to create safe, diverse, healthy, inclusive and respectful workplaces where humans thrive.

#NotOnMyWatch because it doesn't matter how many accolades or awards you or your organisation receives, what matters is what *you* do, or don't do. The culture of your workplace is shaped by the worst behaviour you tolerate as its leader.

ACKNOWLEDGEMENTS

For a solid decade I have been joking about writing 'the book'. While it seemed like a lovely aspiration, my extremely full work and home life and depleting energy levels really made it seem like the impossible dream. Somehow, one day, I decided to put pen to paper in a hair-dressing salon (of all places) to capture some ideas floating around in my head. That was the beginning of a very long work in progress.

I reached out and spoke to a few friends who knew a thing or two about this 'book business' that I clearly had no idea about. I thank them for their support and generosity to get this off the ground. Dr Kirstin Ferguson, Angela Priestly, Marina Go and Tracey Spicer – I am honoured to know you and so humbled by your support. You are incredible women with very full lives and yet contribute so much to make the lives of other women better and to amplify their talents and achievements. Thank you for taking time out of your busy schedules to give me guidance, direction and support. I am indebted to you all and hope we can make some impact in creating the change we all agree we need to see.

To Ryan McGrory – thank you for your time and insights for the book. I look forward to reading your book and working with you to make workplaces safe. Your work is necessary. Your good humour makes it fun and engaging. That is a rare combo in the safety space. It will be your superpower.

To Lisa Annese and Diversity Council of Australia – thank you for the incredible and necessary work you do. I am so grateful for your generosity in sharing so many insights, unique and progressive perspectives for this book. I love your work and value our partnership to change our little corners of the world together. Thank you for the opportunity to share a very small part of DCA's work in this book – although the short grabs do not do justice to the extensive and well-researched reports you produce.

To Walkley Award–winning journalist Catherine Fox AM – I cannot believe you said yes to an interview. I have 'fangirled' over you since I read *Stop Fixing Women*, and never in my wildest dreams did I think you would do me the honour of contributing to a book I wrote. I am so grateful for the time and the perspectives you have so generously and graciously shared. Thank you so much for your contribution and your tireless efforts in making our world a better place for women.

To my parents – there are no words for the sacrifices you have made and the adversity you have suffered, or to describe the incredible humans you both are. I am so very proud to be your daughter and so proud to share the milestone of publishing this book with you. You are both my heroes. Everything I aspire to be as a human and so much more. I may be Fay Calderone on the cover, but I will always be Fotini Savvides at heart.

To my sister – yes, it is hard waking up every day and giving 110 per cent to everything I do. I took your little observation and turned it into a book because that's what overachievers do! Also: since we had that little exchange, it seems you've stepped it up 200 per cent in the parenting stakes and I am so proud of you – all that you have endured and shown incredible courage and strength through. I love you and your boys so much.

To my husband Peter – thank you for your support and belief in me and for being the most amazing father to our boys. We didn't have the time and space to cover the world of neurodivergence that you know better than anyone after two decades of tireless work, study and advocacy. I am told to always leave something for the next book and that certainly looks like a plan with a co-author in my life partner.

Finally, to my gorgeous, loud, funny, talented and relentlessly exhausting boys Elijah and Christian. I adore you both. Thank you for giving me the time and space to fulfill my dream of writing this book when I could have been hanging out with you and doing 'fun stuff' (Elijah especially). I hope one day you both look back and understand my obsession for writing this and the significance of what I am writing. I hope you follow my lead and chase your dreams. Elijah – I live vicariously through you every time you perform with that angelic voice of yours. Chase that dream and chase it hard along with the many others you will have along the way. You are a little superstar. I love your enthusiasm for life and eternal optimism. I love life when I am living it with you and watching it through your eyes. Christian – you already know what it means to chase a dream. You focus with a ball at your feet rather than a pen in your hand, but the sky is the limit with your dedication, commitment, discipline and drive. I am so proud of you and the man you have become. Success is the best revenge. Life is not about avoiding setbacks; it's about finding the strength to rise each time you stumble, forging resilience even when you feel broken.

And to everyone who picked up a copy of *Broken to Safe* – thank you. I am honoured and truly humbled that you took the time. I hope it helps make your workplace better and the humans around you safer.

ABOUT THE AUTHOR

Fay is a reputable employment lawyer with over 20 years' experience assisting employers ensure workplace health and safety and manage performance and conduct issues in the workplace including bullying, discrimination and sexual harassment claims. As a trusted adviser to leaders and HR professionals navigating the complex landscape of employment law, Fay provides pragmatic solutions to the myriad challenges faced by organisations, while nurturing positive workplace cultures.

Known for her expertise and thought leadership, Fay delivers engaging training sessions to boards, leaders and HR professionals transcending beyond mere legal compliance, to the creation of safe, respectful, inclusive and high performing workplaces. A prominent figure in national discussions surrounding critical workplace issues, Fay generously contributes to industry publications, actively engages her professional network on social media, provides commentary to mainstream media and delivers thought provoking keynotes and presentations focused on inspiring positive change.

A prolific writer and speaker drawing insights from day to day practice, Fay possesses an insatiable curiosity about the human condition and how it manifests in the workplace. Her overarching purpose remains steadfast: to assist leaders create workplaces that are not only legally compliant but inherently safer, more inclusive and respectful for every human.

WHAT'S NEXT

Thank you for investing your time in *Broken to Safe*. I trust that the insights shared have inspired you to champion positive trans-formations within your workplace. I am eager to hear how you've implemented these strategies and the impacts they've had. Connect and share your experiences with me:

Reach Out to Fay Calderone

🌐 book.brokentosafe.com.au

in @FayCalderone

♪ @BrokentoSafe

📷 @BrokentoSafe

𝕏 @FayCalderone

Engage Further with Fay Calderone

I am excited to work with you to create a safer and more inclusive workplace. Here are some ways we can continue to drive meaningful change together:

1. **KEYNOTES:** Inspiring talks tailored to energise leaders and teams towards embracing safe and inclusive workplaces.

2. **EXECUTIVE TRAINING:** Specialised sessions for boards, leaders and HR professionals aimed at not only ensuring legal compliance but deepening understanding and skills in creating safe, inclusive and respectful work environments.

3. **POLICY DEVELOPMENT:** Assistance in crafting tailored and robust policies, procedures, and risk management frameworks that reinforce your commitment to a safe and inclusive workplace.

4. **COMPLAINTS MANAGEMENT:** Expert guidance on handling investigations and managing complaints related to unlawful conduct effectively.

5. **STRATEGIC ADVICE ON EXITING PERPETRATORS:** Consultations focused on the sensitive aspects of removing perpetrators from the workplace while minimising legal and reputational risks.

6. **TAILORED WORKPLACE SOLUTIONS:** Customised advice to ensure your workplace is not only legally compliant but safe, inclusive and high performing.

REFERENCES

1   Catherine Fox, https://catherinefox.com.au.
2   Australian Human Rights Commission (2020), *Respect@Work: Sexual Harassment National Inquiry Report*, https://humanrights.gov.au/our-work/sex-discrimination/publications/respectwork-sexual-harassment-national-inquiry-report-2020.
3   Deloitte (2023), *2023 Gen Z and Millennial Survey*, www2.deloitte.com/content/dam/Deloitte/si/Documents/deloitte-2023-genz-millennial-survey.pdf.
4   Safe Work Australia (2022), *Model Code of Practice: Managing psychosocial hazards at work*, https://www.safeworkaustralia.gov.au/sites/default/files/2022-08/model_code_of_practice_-_managing_psychosocial_hazards_at_work_25082022_0.pdf.
5   Our Watch (2024), 'New campaign to end sexual harassment at work', www.ourwatch.org.au/resource/new-campaign-to-end-sexual-harassment-at-work.
6   Ibid.
7   Ibid.
8   Ibid.
9   Plan International 2023, 'Until we are all equal', www.plan.org.au/media-centre/until-we-are-all-equal-plan-international-australia-releases-gender-compass-a-first-of-its-kind-study-revealing-what-ordinary-australians-really-think-about-gender-equality.
10 Michael Timms (2022), 'Blame Culture Is Toxic. Here's How to Stop It', *Harvard Business Review*, https://hbr.org/2022/02/blame-culture-is-toxic-heres-how-to-stop-it.

11 Science Direct (n.d.), 'Adaptation syndrome – an overview', www.sciencedirect.com/topics/immunology-and-microbiology/adaptation-syndrome.

12 Northwestern Medicine (2020), '5 Things You Never Knew About Fear', www.nm.org/healthbeat/healthy-tips/emotional-health/5-things-you-never-knew-about-fear.

13 Jaime Rosenberg (2017), 'The Effects of Chronic Fear on a Person's Health', *The American Journal of Managed Care*, www.ajmc.com/view/the-effects-of-chronic-fear-on-a-persons-health.

14 Australian Human Rights Commission and the Respect@Work Council (n.d.), *Respect@Work*, www.respectatwork.gov.au.

15 Ibid.

16 Ibid.

17 Ibid.

18 Mary Slaughter, Khalil Smith and David Rock (2018), 'The Brain Science That Could Help Explain Sexual Harassment', *Psychology Today*, www.psychologytoday.com/ie/blog/your-brain-at-work/201802/the-brain-science-that-could-help-explain-sexual-harassment.

19 Seiara Imanova (2022), 'Neuroscience of Mental Health – The Effects of Workplace Bullying', Applied Neuroscience Association, https://appliedneuroscienceassociation.com/2022/11/16/neuroscience-of-mental-health-the-effects-of-workplace-bullying.

20 Ibid.

21 Ibid.

22 Laura Delizonna (2017), 'High-Performing Teams Need Psychological Safety: Here's How to Create It', Harvard Business Review, https://hbr.org/2017/08/high-performing-teams-need-psychological-safety-heres-how-to-create-it.

23 Michael Timms, op. cit.

24 Michael Timms, op. cit.

25 Gallup (n.d.), 'Strengths Development & Coaching', www.gallup.com/learning/248405/strengths-development-coaching.aspx.

26 Ibid.

27 Michelle McQuaid (2023), *The Leaders Lab 2023 Australia Workplace Report*, The Leaders Lab, www.michellemcquaid.com/theleaderslab/2023research.

28 Kenneth M Nowack and Paul J Zak (2020), 'In Team We Trust', *Talent Quarterly*, www.talent-quarterly.com/in-team-we-trust.

29 Mental Health First Aid Australia (n.d.), 'Navigating burnout', www.mhfa.com.au/navigating-burnout.

30 ReachOut Australia (n.d.), 'What is burnout?', https://au.reachout.com/articles/what-is-burnout.

31 DAJ Salvagioni et al. (2017), 'Physical, psychological and occupational consequences of job burnout: A systematic review of prospective studies', *PLoS One*, 12(10). /

32 Ibid.

33 Nien-hê Hsieh (2023), 'Ethical Analysis: Foundations', Harvard Business School Background Note 324-059, www.hbs.edu/faculty/Pages/item.aspx?num=65010.

34 World Health Organization (WHO; 2022), 'Mental health at work', www.who.int/news-room/fact-sheets/detail/mental-health-at-work.

35 Michelle McQuaid, op. cit.

36 Ben Wigert and Sangeeta Agrawal (2018), 'Employee Burnout, Part 1: The 5 Main Causes', Gallup, www.gallup.com/workplace/237059/employee-burnout-part-main-causes.aspx.

37 Lisa Earle McLeod and Elizabeth Lotardo (2023), 'How to Be a Purpose-Driven Leader Without Burning Out', *Harvard Business Review*, https://hbr.org/2023/07/how-to-be-a-purpose-driven-leader-without-burning-out.

38 Lisa Earle McLeod and Elizabeth Lotardo, op. cit.

39 Ibid.

40 Ibid.

41 Ibid.

42 Exsona (n.d), 'Our team', www.exsona.com/our-team.

43 Australian Bureau of Statistics (2023), 'National Study of Mental Health and Wellbeing', www.abs.gov.au/statistics/health/mental-health/national-study-mental-health-and-wellbeing/latest-release.

44 Safe Work Australia (2024), Snapshot: Psychological health and safety in the workplace, https://data.safeworkaustralia.gov.au/sites/default/files/2024-02/Psychological-health-in-the-workplace_Snapshot_February 2024.pdf.

45 Safe Work Australia (2022), op. cit.

46 Ibid.

47 Safe Work Australia (2016), *Psychosocial Safety Climate and Better Productivity in Australian Workplaces: Cost, Productivity, Presenteeism, Absenteeism*, https://www.safeworkaustralia.gov.au/system/files/documents/1705/psychosocial-safety-climate-and-better-productivity-in-australian-workplaces-nov-2016.pdf.

48 WorkSafe Victoria (2023), 'Court body fined almost $380,000 for deadly work culture', www.worksafe.vic.gov.au/news/2023-10/court-body-fined-almost-380000-deadly-work-culture.

49 Ibid.

50 Ibid.

51 Ibid.

52 SafeWork NSW v Marist Youth Care Limited [2024] NSWDC 74

53 Safe Work Australia (2016), *Guide for Preventing and Responding to Workplace Bullying*, www.safeworkaustralia.gov.au/system/files/documents/1702/guide-preventing-responding-workplace-bullying.pdf.

54 Ibid.

55 Carol Dweck (2017), *Mindset: Changing the way you think to fulfill your potential*, Robinson.

56 Emma Seppälä (2015), 'Why Compassion Is a Better Managerial Tactic than Toughness', *Harvard Business Review*, https://hbr.org/2015/05/why-compassion-is-a-better-managerial-tactic-than-toughness.

57 Ibid.

58 https://www.ourwatch.org.au/resource/telling-and-changing-the-story-of-violence-against-women/

59 The Red Heart Campaign (n.d.), https://australianfemicidewatch.org.

60 Annabel Crabb (2015), 'I'm proud to be a feminist despite my regular lapses', *The Sydney Morning Herald*, www.smh.com.au/opinion/annabel-crabb-im-proud-to-be-a-feminist-despite-my-regular-lapses-20150306-13wrw2.html.

61 Holly Wainwright (2023), 'Another Good Bloke', *Mamamia*, www.mamamia.com.au/the-good-bloke-effect.

62 Ibid.

63 McNicol, E., Fitz-Gibbon, K. and Brewer, S. (2022), 'From workplace sabotage to embedded supports: examining the impact of domestic and family violence across Australian workplaces', Monash University.

64 Ibid.

65 Ibid.

66 Ibid.

67 Ibid.

68 Ibid.

69 Safe Work Australia (n.d.), 'Family and domestic violence at the workplace', www.safeworkaustralia.gov.au/sites/default/files/2021-01/family_and_domestic_violence_information_sheet.pdf.

70 Jess Hill (2019), *See What You Made Me Do: Power, Control and Domestic Abuse*, Black Inc.

71 Malcolm Turnbull (2015), Facebook, www.facebook.com/malcolmturnbull/photos/disrespecting-women-doesnt-always-result-in-violence-against-women-but-all-viole/10153721624181579/?_rdr.

72 Safe Work Australia (2022), 'Managing psychosocial hazards at work', www.safeworkaustralia.gov.au/sites/default/files/2022-09/managing_psychosocial_hazards_at_work.pdf.

73 Ibid.

74 Australian Human Rights Commission (2023), *Guidelines for Complying with the Positive Duty under the Sex Discrimination Act 1984 (Cth)*, https://humanrights.gov.au/sites/default/files/2023-08/Guidelines%20for%20Complying%20with%20the%20Positive%20Duty%20%282023%29.pdf.

75 Australian Human Rights Commission (2023), Person-centred and Trauma-informed Approaches to Safe and Respectful Workplaces, https://humanrights.gov.au/sites/default/files/factsheet_-_person-centred_and_trauma-informed_approaches_to_safe_and_respectful_workplaces_0.pdf.

76 *Richardson v Oracle Corporation Australia Pty Ltd* [2014] FCAFC 82.

77 *Hill v Hughes [2019]* FCCA 1267.

78 *Homer Abarra v Toyota Motor Corporation Australia Ltd [2018]* FWC 2761.

79 *Taylor v Startrack Express [2017]* FWC 6083.

80 John Tamaliunas v Alcoa of Australia Limited [2024] FWC 779

81 Dr Pragya Agarwal (2018), 'How To Create A Positive Workplace Culture', *Forbes*, www.forbes.com/sites/pragyaagarwaleurope/2018/08/29/how-to-create-a-positive-work-place-culture/?sh=34ded9284272.

82 Safety Solutions (2012), 'Half of Australia's workers would rather quit than deal with workplace issues', www.safetysolutions.net.au/content/business/article/half-of-australia-rsquo-s-workers-would-rather-quit-than-deal-with-workplace-issues-1101052309.

83 Leading with Trust (2018), 'The Leadership Superpower That Builds Trust and Connection', https://leadingwithtrust.com/2018/07/08/the-leadership-superpower-that-builds-trust-and-connection.

84 Chase Thiel et al. (2024), 'Surveilling Employees Erodes Trust — and Puts Managers in a Bind', Harvard Business Review, https://hbr.org/2024/02/surveilling-employees-erodes-trust-and-puts-managers-in-a-bind.

85 Paul J Zak (2017), 'The Neuroscience of Trust', *Harvard Business Review*, https://hbr.org/2017/01/the-neuroscience-of-trust.

86 Kenneth M Nowack and Paul J Zak (2020), 'In Team We Trust', *Talent Quarterly*, www.talent-quarterly.com/in-team-we-trust.

87 Ibid.

88 Phoebe Armstrong (2024), 'How can HR help build trust in the workplace?', *HRM*, www.hrmonline.com.au/section/featured/build-trust-in-the-workplace.

89 CEDA (2024), 'Remote work has boosted employment for parents and people with a disability', www.ceda.com.au/newsandresources/

mediareleases/economy/remote-work-has-boosted-employment-for-parents-and-people-with-a-disability.

90 Ibid.

91 Cal Newport (2016), *Deep Work: Rules for Focused Success in a Distracted World*, Grand Central Publishing.

92 OECD (2020), 'Productivity gains from teleworking in the post COVID-19 era: How can public policies make it happen?', https://www.oecd.org/coronavirus/policy-responses/productivity-gains-from-teleworking-in-the-post-covid-19-era-a5d52e99.

93 Ibid.

94 Ibid.

95 Ibid.

96 Ibid.

97 Workplace Gender Equality Agency (2021), 'Flexible work post-COVID', https://www.wgea.gov.au/publications/flexible-work-post-covid.

98 Bain & Company (2016), 'Flexibility For All: Barriers to flexibility still stand in the way of gender parity', bain.com/about/media-center/press-releases/2016/australia-gender-parity-report-2016-press-release.

99 Ibid.

100 Workplace Gender Equality Agency (2023), 'WGEA Gender Equality Scorecard 2022-23', https://www.wgea.gov.au/publications/australias-gender-equality-scorecard.

101 Catherine Fox (2017), *Stop Fixing Women: Why building fairer workplaces is everybody's business*, NewSouth.

102 Sharon Klyne (2023), 'Managing the toll of menopause', *Investment Magazine*, www.investmentmagazine.com.au/2023/01/managing-the-toll-of-menopause.

103 Ibid.

104 Hannah Hickok (2021), 'Are men-dominated offices the future of the workplace?', BBC, www.bbc.com/worklife/article/20210503-are-men-dominated-offices-the-future-of-the-workplace.

105 Michael Bleby (2020), 'More men want to return to the office than women', Australian Financial Review, www.afr.com/property/commercial/more-men-want-to-return-to-the-office-than-women-20201117-p56fi4.

106 Bain & Company, op. cit.

107 Workplace Gender Equality Agency (2019), 'Employers should set targets for men in flexible work & help dads manage the juggle: Libby Lyons', www.wgea.gov.au/newsroom/employers-should-set-targets-for-men-in-flexible-work-help-dads-manage-the-juggle-libby-lyons.

108 Ibid.

109 Diversity Council Australia (2023), 'New study finds workplace inclusion & flexibility can improve mental health', www.dca.org.au/news/media-releases/workplace-inclusion-flexibility-can-improve-mental-health?at_context=905.

110 Beyond Blue (n.d.) 'Men', www.beyondblue.org.au/who-does-it-affect/men.

111 Workplace Gender Equality Agency, op. cit.

112 PwC (2021), *The Future of Work, What Workers Want: Winning the War for Talent*,https://www.pwc.com.au/important-problems/future-of-work/what-workers-want-report.pdf.

113 Deloitte (2023), *2023 Gen Z and Millennial Survey*, https://www.deloitte.com/global/en/issues/work/content/genzmillennialsurvey.html.

114 Vanessa Vanderhoek (2017), 'The perception problem with flexible work needs addressing', *Women's Agenda*, https://womensagenda.com.au/life/jugglehood/perception-problem-flexible-work-needs-addressing-today.

115 Millie Muroi (2023), 'Working from home will be history in three years' time, CEOs predict', *The Sydney Morning Herald*, www.smh.com.au/business/companies/working-from-home-will-be-history-in-three-years-time-ceos-predict-20231005-p5e9x8.html.

116 David Swan (2024), 'Companies will regret return-to-office mandates', *The Sydney Morning Herald*, https://www.smh.com.au/business/workplace/companies-will-regret-return-to-office-mandates-atlassian-20240117-p5exvb.html.

117 Atlassian (2024), *Lessons learned: 1,000 days of distributed at Atlassian*, www.atlassian.com/blog/distributed-work/distributed-work-report.

118 Diversity Council Australia (2024), Inclusion@Work Index 2023–24, https://www.dca.org.au/research/inclusion-at-work-index-2023-2024.

119 Ibid.

120 Ibid.

121 Ibid.

122 Ibid.

123 Juliet Bourke and Andrea Titus (2020), 'The Key to Inclusive Leadership', *Harvard Business Review*, https://hbr.org/2020/03/the-key-to-inclusive-leadership.

124 Ibid.

125 Diversity Council Australia (2020), *Class at Work*, www.dca.org.au/research/class-at-work.

126 Ibid.

127 Terry Fitzsimmons (2011), 'Navigating CEO appointments: Do Australia's top male and female CEOs differ in how they reached the top?' PhD thesis. Brisbane: The University of Queensland.

128 Ibid.

129 Diversity Council Australia (2023), 'Words at Work: Should we use CALD or CARM?', www.dca.org.au/news/blog/words-at-work-should-we-use-cald-or-carm.

130 Karyn Twaronite (2019), 'The Surprising Power of Simply Asking Coworkers How They're Doing', *Harvard Business Review*, https://hbr.org/2019/02/the-surprising-power-of-simply-asking-coworkers-how-theyre-doing.

131 Evan Carr et al. (2019), ''The Value of Belonging at Work', '*Harvard Business Review*, https://hbr.org/2019/12/the-value-of-belonging-at-work.

132 Ibid.

133 Tomas Chamorro-Premuzic (2020), 'How to Spot an Incompetent Leader', *Harvard Business Review*, https://hbr.org/2020/03/how-to-spot-an-incompetent-leader.

134 Donald Sull and Charles Sull (2022), 'How to Fix a Toxic Culture', *MIT Sloan Management Review*, https://sloanreview.mit.edu/article/how-to-fix-a-toxic-culture.

135 Ibid.

136 Ibid.

137 Ibid.

138 Perry Belcher, https://www.linkedin.com/in/perrybelcher.

139 Donald Sull and Charles Sull, op. cit.

140 Steve Gruenert and Todd Whitaker (2015), *School Culture Rewired*.

141 *Sex Discrimination Act 1984* (Cth).

www.ingramcontent.com/pod-product-compliance
Lightning Source LLC
Chambersburg PA
CBHW071211210326
41597CB00016B/1762